Thesis and Dissertation Writing in a Second Language

The changing demographics of higher education in conjunction with imperatives of greater accountability and increasing support for research students mean that many supervisors find themselves challenged by the task of guiding non-native-speaker students to completion.

Thesis and Dissertation Writing in a Second Language is a practical guide containing useful real-life examples. Tasks in each unit are designed for supervisors to use with their students to help them develop the skills and understanding necessary for successful thesis and dissertation writing.

Each unit of the book focuses on a particular aspect of thesis and dissertation writing and the research and supervision process, including:

- aspects of language use particular to thesis and dissertation writing;
- typical chapter structures and organization;
- social and cultural expectations particular to writing a thesis or dissertation;
- what is expected of students in this kind of writing and at this level of study;
- expectations of students and supervisors in the supervision and thesis writing process;
- disciplinary differences in thesis writing;
- what examiners expect of theses and dissertations written in English-medium universities;
- insights into barriers faced by non-native-speaking students studying for a research degree.

Thesis and Dissertation Writing in a Second Language is the ideal guide for all supervisors working with non-native-speaker students writing a thesis or dissertation in English. This accessible text provides guidelines to facilitate successful writing using tasks which encourage students to apply the points covered in each unit to their own situation.

Brian Paltridge is Associate Professor of TESOL at the University of Sydney in Australia. **Sue Starfield** is Director of the Learning Centre, and a Visiting Fellow in the Department of Linguistics, University of New South Wales. They both have extensive experience in working with students writing a thesis or dissertation in English as their second language.

D0273806

Thesis and Dissertation Writing in a Second Language

A handbook for supervisors

Brian Paltridge and Sue Starfield

Routledge
Taylor & Francis Group

LONDON AND NEW YORK

First published 2007 by Routledge
2 Park Square, Milton Park, Abingdon, Oxon, OX14 4RN

Simultaneously published in the USA and Canada
by Routledge
270 Madison Ave, New York, NY 10016

Routledge is an imprint of the Taylor & Francis Group, an informa business

© 2007 Brian Paltridge and Sue Starfield

Typeset in Garamond by
GreenGate Publishing Services, Tonbridge, Kent
Printed and bound in Great Britain by Antony Rowe Ltd, Chippenham, Wiltshire.

British Library Cataloguing in Publication Data
A catalogue record for this book is available from the British Library

Library of Congress Cataloging in Publication Data
Paltridge, Brian.
    Thesis and dissertation writing in a second language : a handbook for
supervisors / Brian Paltridge and Sue Starfield.
        p. cm.
    Includes bibliographical references and index.
    ISBN 978-0-415-37170-4 (alk. paper) -- ISBN 978-0-415-37173-5 (pbk. : alk.
paper) 1. Dissertations, Academic--Authorship. 2. Academic writing. 3. English
language--Study and teaching--Foreign speakers. I. Starfield, Sue, 1952- II. Title.
    LB2369.P353 2007
    808'.042--dc22
    2006038301

ISBN10: 0–415–37170–8 (hbk)
ISBN10: 0–415–37173–2 (pbk)
ISBN10: 0–203–96081–5 (ebk)

ISBN13: 978–0–415–37170–4 (hbk)
ISBN13: 978–0–415–37173–5 (pbk)
ISBN13: 978–0–203–96081–3 (ebk)

Contents

Illustrations

Figures

Tables

Boxes

Acknowledgements

This book is the result of many years of teaching, talking and thinking about thesis and dissertation writing with our students, colleagues, friends and families. We thank them all. We would also like to acknowledge the many doctoral and master's students whose theses have contributed extracts to this book. Specifically we would like to thank Dwight Atkinson, Diane Belcher, Chris Casanave, Andy Curtis, Tony Dudley-Evans, Chris Feak, Liz Hamp-Lyons, Alan Hirvela, Cynthia Nelson, Louise Ravelli and John Swales for their interest, support and inspiration; Tracey-Lee Downey for her help with illustrations; our anonymous reviewers as well as Philip Mudd at RoutledgeFalmer for his support for our project and Lucy Wainwright, also at RoutledgeFalmer, for seeing our project through to completion.

Being able to develop and teach our courses in thesis and dissertation writing has been and continues to be a rewarding experience for us both. From what our students tell us, they find the courses very helpful with the development of their own writing. Writing a research thesis in a language that is not your native one is undoubtedly a challenge. We hope that other students and their supervisors will find our book helpful in meeting that challenge and that the students' unique contribution to knowledge in their field will be enhanced.

Sue would especially like to acknowledge her parents for their unconditional love and support and thank Alan, Sophia and Jeremy for putting up with her during the writing process. She would also like to thank Adrian Lee and Richard Henry for their encouragement and her Learning Centre colleagues for being passionate about writing. Brian would like to acknowledge the support he has in his faculty for the work that he does, and his colleagues and research students there for making it the place to be that it is.

Chapter 1

Introduction

Background to the book

The aim of this book is to provide a handbook for supervisors who are working with students writing a thesis or dissertation[1] in English as their second language. The book aims to unpack some of the tacit understanding that supervisors often have of the thesis or dissertation writing process that is often not shared by their students, and in this case, students who come from a language and culture background other than English. The book is also suitable for teachers who run courses or workshops on thesis and dissertation writing for second-language students. There are practical examples, learning tasks, and examples from completed theses and dissertations throughout the book. The learning tasks are designed to help students develop the skills and understandings necessary for successful thesis and dissertation writing. These learning tasks include a focus on aspects of language use particular to thesis and dissertation writing, as well as the social and cultural expectations particular to writing a thesis or dissertation, such as what is expected of students in this kind of writing and at this level of study, expectations of students and supervisors in the supervision and thesis writing process, the issue of disciplinary differences in thesis writing, and what examiners expect of theses and dissertations written in English-medium universities.

The book includes a focus on theory and research, where appropriate, as well as providing practical advice on thesis and dissertation writing for second-language students. It discusses issues that are common to all thesis and dissertation writers, such as understanding the setting and purpose of thesis and dissertation writing, the place of audience in thesis and dissertation writing, understanding writer/reader relationships, issues of writer identity, and the place of assumed background knowledge in thesis and dissertation writing.

Each unit of the book focuses on a particular aspect of thesis and dissertation writing and the research and supervision process. The sequencing of the units follows the stages of carrying out research and writing a thesis or dissertation. Each of the units includes tasks for supervisors to use with their students. The tasks are written in a way that encourages students to explore the points that are covered in each chapter in relation to their own discipline-specific and academic situation.

While there are a large number of texts that offer support to students with assignment writing, there are far fewer that offer support to students who are writing a thesis or dissertation. Furthermore, assignment writing is a quantitatively and qualitatively different task to writing a thesis or dissertation and managing the writing process over a sustained period of time. There are a number of books that offer advice to research students but very few of these provide detailed instruction in the writing of the actual thesis and hardly any offer specific advice to students from non-English-speaking backgrounds (see Paltridge 2002 for further discussion of this).

We hope that the approach to the conceptualizing and teaching of thesis and dissertation writing presented in this book will be of benefit to our disciplinary colleagues. The approach adopted is one which explicitly teaches the expectations, conventions, structure and organization of the various sections of the typical thesis and dissertation. It also draws on authentic instances of theses and dissertations to illustrate these features of the texts. While the aim of this book is to make the issues we discuss clear to second-language students and their supervisors, there is much in this book that will also be of use to native-speaker students, and to students who have already studied in an English-medium university but have not previously written a text of the kind we are discussing.

Background to thesis and dissertation writing in a second language

A large number of second-language students attending British, US, Canadian, Australian and New Zealand universities are enrolled in a degree that requires the writing of a thesis or dissertation in English. There are also many students enrolled in degrees in places such as South Africa and Hong Kong who are required to write a thesis or dissertation in English for whom English is not their first or dominant language. Such students often have difficulty in meeting the demands of the kind of writing required of them in this particular genre. This is especially the case for students who come from a context where the conventions and expectations of academic writing may be quite different to the situation they now find themselves in.

This chapter discusses:

- the context in which theses and dissertations are produced and the implications of this for second-language writers from diverse linguistic and cultural backgrounds;
- the very particular social and cultural context of theses and dissertations and how this impacts on what students write and how they can write it;
- approaches to knowledge and approaches to learning at different levels of study;

- cross-cultural issues in thesis and dissertation writing;
- the issue of being a second-language writer in research settings;
- critical issues in thesis and dissertation writing;
- disciplinary differences in thesis and dissertation writing;
- what universities and examiners expect of theses and dissertations.

The social and cultural context of thesis and dissertation writing

We have found that a useful way to discuss thesis and dissertation writing with our students is by starting with an examination of the social and cultural context in which the student's thesis or dissertation is being produced. Factors that might be discussed with the student, for example, include:

- the setting of the text;
- the focus and perspective of the text;
- the purpose/s of the text;
- the intended audience for the text, their role and purpose in reading the text;
- the relationship between writers and readers of the text;
- expectations, conventions and requirements for the text;
- the background knowledge, values, and understandings it is assumed the student shares with their readers, including what is important to their reader and what is not;
- the relationship the text has with other texts.

Each of these is important to consider as they all, in their way, have an impact on what the student writes and the way they write it. Often these issues are mutually understood by people working in the university, but not explicitly stated to students. This discussion can include values and expectations that are held in a particular area of study, the audience students are writing for, and different expectations at different levels of study. We have found it useful to have this discussion with students before they start writing their thesis or dissertation, as well as before we look at examples of actual texts with them. Some of the issues we raise with our students are discussed below.

The setting of the students' text

The setting of the student's text includes the kind of university and level of study the thesis or dissertation is being written in. This may be a comprehensive research university, or it may be a university of technology where different sorts of work and different sorts of research projects might be more especially valued. The thesis or dissertation may be being written for an honours, a master's, or a doctoral degree. This has implications for the breadth and scale of the student's research project.

Another important issue is the kind of study area the student's text is being written in; that is, whether it is written in what Becher and Trowler (2001) call a 'hard' or a 'soft' discipline, a 'pure' or 'applied' discipline, or a 'convergent' or 'divergent' area of study. This has important implications for understanding the values, ideologies and research perspectives that are prioritized in the students' area/s of study. Students can be asked, for example, to consider whether academic staff in their area of study share the same basic ideologies, judgments and values (a convergent area of study) or whether their research perspectives are drawn from other areas of study (a divergent area of study). They might consider whether there is more variation in what might be considered 'research' in their particular area of study, and to what extent this makes a difference as to what students can 'say' and do. This discussion helps students to place their dissertation in its particular academic setting as well as to bring to the fore the sets of values that hold in their area of study that might be shared by members of academic staff, but not openly expressed by them.

Research perspective, topic and purpose of the thesis or dissertation

Students can be asked to consider the research perspective and topic of their research project and the extent to which this impacts on how they will write their thesis or dissertation. They can consider, for example, whether they are doing a quantitative or qualitative study or whether their research project is an example of 'mixed method' research, and what particular assumptions these perspectives imply. This includes what sorts of claims can be made in the particular perspective and area of study, and what claims cannot.

Students can then be asked to consider the actual purpose of their research, and in turn, their thesis or dissertation. This may, for example, be to answer a question, to solve a problem, or to prove something, as well as to contribute to knowledge in their area of study. The purpose may equally be to display knowledge and understanding of a particular topic, to demonstrate particular skills, to convince a reader, as well as, often, to 'gain admission to a particular area of study'. Students are often required in this kind of writing not only to answer their research question/s, but also to 'show what they know' in doing this (see Chapters 3, 5 and 6 where this is discussed in more detail).

The audience for theses and dissertations

A further issue that students should consider is the intended audience for their thesis or dissertation, their readers' role and purpose in reading their text, how their readers will react to what they read, and the criteria they will use for assessing their text. For example, are the students writing for academics in the field, for their examiners, or for their supervisor? And who counts most in judging whether their text meets the requirements of their particular area of study?

Theses and dissertations are typically written for a primary readership of one or more examiners. In some cases the student's supervisor may be one of the examiners and in other cases they may not. If the supervisor is not one of the student's examiners, they will be a secondary reader of the student's text, not a primary one. This difference between 'primary' and 'secondary' readerships (Brookes and Grundy 1990) is significant, and is often not immediately obvious to students. In the case of thesis and dissertation writing, it is the primary reader that is the final judge as to the quality of the student's piece of work, rather than the secondary reader. As Kamler and Threadgold (1997: 53) point out, a dominant or 'primary' reader within the academy, 'quite simply counts more than other readers' (such as friends, learning advisors and anyone else the student shows their text to). It is important, then, for students to consider the expert, 'all-powerful reader' of their texts who can either accept, or reject, their writing as being coherent and consistent with the conventions of the target discourse community (Johns 1990) and how they will (potentially) read their text.

The relationship between writers and readers of theses and dissertations

Next, students can be asked to consider the relationship between their readers and themselves as writers and how this impacts on what they say and how they can say it. They can also be asked to consider how this relationship changes for other academic texts such as research articles and conference presentations. Writers of theses and dissertations, for example, are typically 'novices writing for experts' whereas writers of research articles are generally 'experts writing for experts'. Conference presentations, for research students, are often a mix of the two.

Background knowledge, values and understandings in thesis and dissertation writing

Another useful topic to discuss is the background knowledge, values, and understandings it is assumed students will share with their primary readers (their examiners), what is important to their readers, and what is not. This, students will discover, impacts on how much 'display of knowledge' their text should contain, to what extent they should 'show what they know', as well as what issues they should address, what boundaries they can cross (Kamler and Threadgold 1997), and how they might do this.

Discourse community expectations and thesis and dissertation writing

It is also useful to discuss general expectations and conventions for theses and dissertations, as well as the particular expectations, conventions and requirements of the students' area of study. Students can be asked how a thesis or dissertation might typically be organized and how this might vary for a particular research topic and kind of study.

The next issue is what might typically be contained in each chapter of the thesis or dissertation and what amount of variation might be allowed in all of this. A further important topic is the level of critical analysis required of students at the particular level and area of study and the level of originality and 'contribution to knowledge' expected of the students' research projects.

Relationship with other texts

A final important point to discuss with students is the relationship their thesis or dissertation has with other texts such as monographs, journal articles and research reports, as well as how they are expected to show the relationship between what they are writing and what others have written before them on their topic. Students can be asked how they might use other texts to support arguments they wish to make, as well as differences between acceptable and unacceptable textual borrowings (Pennycook 1996) and differences between reporting and plagiarizing.

The context of theses and dissertations

Table 1.1 (see p.8) is an analysis of the social and cultural context of theses and dissertations based on this set of questions. This table shows the range of factors that impact on how a student's text is written, how it will be read and, importantly, how it will be assessed.

Applications

1   Ask your student to consider the following in relation to their thesis or dissertation. To what extent do these factors influence what they write and how they write it?

   * the institutional setting of the text;
   * the focus and perspective of the text;
   * the intended audience for the text.

2   Ask your student to consider how these factors influence how they write their text:

- university expectations, conventions and requirements for the thesis or dissertation;
- the background knowledge, values, and understandings it is assumed they will share with their readers, including what is important to their readers and what is not.

3   Ask your student to discuss the differences between reporting, paraphrasing and plagiarizing. Ask what strategies they use when they are paraphrasing other writers' work (see Bailey 2003: 21–22 for a useful activity on paraphrasing).

Attitudes to knowledge and different levels of study

A further useful topic to discuss with students is attitudes to knowledge, learning approaches, and teaching and learning strategies at different levels of study – also how these are often different in English-medium universities from those in second-language-speaker students' own counties. Ballard and Clanchy (1984, 1997) discuss each of these, including how they change as students progress in their studies. For example, the primary focus in an English secondary school education is often 'conserving' knowledge whereas, as a student continues on to tertiary studies, there is often a shift to critiquing and 'extending' knowledge. This may entail a shift from a focus on correctness, to 'simple' originality and, in turn, to 'creative' originality and the creation of new knowledge. Students, thus, often move from summarizing and describing information, to questioning, judging and recombining information, through to a deliberate search for new ideas, data and explanations. Higher levels of study still expect correctness and the recombination of information, however. They also often expect the creation of new knowledge, and a search for new evidence and interpretations (Ballard and Clanchy 1997).

Table 1.2 presents relationships between teaching and learning strategies and attitudes to knowledge at different levels of study in English-medium institutions. This figure is a useful starting point for a discussion with students on these issues, including cross-cultural differences and expectations at different levels of study. Ballard and Clanchy point out, importantly, that the attitudes and strategies they describe are not fixed and static, but on a continuum. In some courses, students vary in the strategies and attitudes to knowledge that they adopt. Equally, the learning strategies students adopt

Table 1.1 The social and cultural context of theses and dissertations

Setting of the text	The kind of university and level of study, the kind of degree (e.g. honours, master's or doctoral, research or professional). Study carried out in a 'hard' or 'soft', pure or applied, convergent or divergent area of study (Becher and Trowler 2001).
Focus and perspective of the text	Quantitative, qualitative or mixed method research. Claims that can be made, claims that cannot be made. Faculty views on what 'good' research is.
Purpose of the text	To answer a question, to solve a problem, to prove something, to contribute to knowledge, to display knowledge and understanding, to demonstrate particular skills, to convince a reader, to gain admission to a particular area of study.
Audience, role and purpose in reading the text	To judge the quality of the research. Primary readership of one or more examiners, secondary readership of everyone else who reads their work. How readers will react to what they read, the criteria they will use for assessing the text, who counts the most in judging the quality of the text.
Relationship between writers and readers of the text	Students writing for experts, for admission to an area of study (the primary readership), students writing for peers, for advice (the secondary readership). Writer identity, authority and positioning.
Expectations, conventions and requirements for the text	An understanding and critical appraisal of relevant literature. A clearly defined and comprehensive investigation of the research topic. Appropriate use of research methods and techniques for the research question. Ability to interpret results, develop conclusions and link them to previous research. Level of critical analysis, originality and contribution to knowledge expected. Literary quality and standard of presentation expected. Level of grammatical accuracy required. How the text is typically organized, how the text might vary for a particular research topic, area of study, kind of study and research perspective. What is typically contained in each chapter. The amount of variation allowed in what should be addressed and how it should be addressed. The university's formal submission requirements in terms of format, procedures and timing.
Background knowledge, values, and understandings	The background knowledge, values, and understandings it is assumed students will share with their readers, what is important to their readers, what is not important to their readers. How much knowledge students are expected to display, the extent to which students should show what they know, what issues students should address, what boundaries students can cross.
Relationship the text has with other texts	How to show the relationship between the present research and other people's research on the topic, what counts as valid previous research, acceptable and unacceptable textual borrowings, differences between reporting and plagiarizing.

Source: Paltridge 2006: 100. By kind permission of Continuum

Table 1.2 Attitudes to knowledge, approaches to learning and different levels of study

Attitudes to knowledge		Conserving knowledge	Critiquing knowledge	Extending knowledge
Learning approaches		Reproductive	Analytical	Speculative
Teaching strategies	Role of the teacher	almost exclusive source of knowledge; direction/ guidance; assessment	coordinator of learning resources; questioner, critical guide, gadfly; principal source of assessment	more experienced colleague and collaborator; preliminary critic and advisor; patron
	Characteristic activities	transmission of information and demonstration of skills; overt moral and social training	analysis of information and ideas within interpretive frameworks; modelling of demand for critical approach to knowledge and conventions	discussion/ advice on ideas and methods on individual basis; modelling of hypothetical and creative thinking
	Assessment	tests of memory recall and practical demonstration of skills; emphasis on replication; geared to ranking	assignment/exams requiring critical analysis and problem solving; emphasis on originality, quality of interpretation	independent research; thesis and papers of publishable quality; contri- bution to field of knowledge
	Aim	simple transfer of knowledge and skills	independent and critical styles of thinking; development of capacity for theory and abstraction	development of speculative, critical intelligence; expansion of knowledge base (theory, data, techniques)
Learning strategies	Type of activities	memorization and imitation; summarizing, describing, identifying, and applying formulae and information	analytical and critical thinking; questioning, judging, and recombining ideas and information into an argument	speculating and hypothesizing; research design, implementation and reporting; deliberate search for new ideas, data, explanations

Table 1.2 continued Attitudes to knowledge, approaches to learning and different levels of study

Attitudes to knowledge		Conserving knowledge	Critiquing knowledge	Extending knowledge
Learning approaches		Reproductive	Analytical	Speculative
	Characteristic questions	what?	why? how? how valid? how important?	What if?
	Aim	correctness	'simple' originality, reshaping material into a different pattern	creative originality, totally new approach/ new knowledge

Source: adapted from Ballard and Clanchy 1997: 12

vary in relation to the different learning tasks they are undertaking. Notwithstanding, English-medium academic institutions often share a dominant set of attitudes towards knowledge and learning strategies that are not immediately apparent to many second-language students writing a thesis or dissertation in English (Ballard and Clanchy 1997).

Application

Discuss Table 1.2 with your student. How similar or different is this to their previous study experiences? For example, which of these character-istics most typically describe their secondary school education? Which most typically describe their undergraduate and postgraduate study? Which of these are important for them to consider in their thesis and dissertation writing?

Cross-cultural issues in thesis and dissertation writing

Writing across cultures

There are a number of cultural issues to consider in thesis and dissertation writing. An important issue is cultural differences in the writing and reading of this kind of academic genre. The area of research known as *contrastive rhetoric* compares writing across languages and cultures. Many studies in this area have focused on academic writing. Contrastive rhetoric has its origins in the work of Kaplan (1966) who examined different patterns in the academic writing of students from a number of different languages and cultures.

Although Kaplan has since revised his strong claim that differences in academic writing are the result of culturally different ways of thinking, many studies have found important differences in the ways in which academic texts are written in different languages and cultures. Other studies, however, have found important similarities in academic writing across cultures. Kubota (1997), for example, argues that studies in the area of contrastive rhetoric tend to overgeneralize the cultural characteristics of writing from a few specific examples. She argues that just as Japanese expository writing, for example, has more than one rhetorical style, so does English, and that it is misleading to try to reduce rhetorical styles to the one single norm.

Leki (1997) has argued that contrastive rhetoric oversimplifies not only other cultures but also ways of writing in English. She points out that while second-language students may often be taught to write in a standard way, professional writers do not necessarily write this way in English. She argues that many rhetorical devices that are said to be typical of Chinese, Japanese and Thai writing, for example, also occur in certain contexts in English. Equally, features that are said to be typical of English writing appear on occasion in other languages as well. Contrastive rhetoric, she argues, can most usefully be seen, not as the study of culture-specific thought patterns, but as the study of 'the differences or preferences in the pragmatic and strategic choices that writers make in response to external demands and cultural histories' (Leki 1997: 244).

Kubota and Lehner (2004) have argued that contrastive rhetoric takes a deficit view of students' second-language academic writing. They also argue that much contrastive rhetoric research presents differences in academic writing that do not always exist. An example of this is the view of Chinese academic writing being circular and indirect and English academic writing being linear and direct. Some Chinese students have said:

> What do you mean when you say English academic writing is linear? In English, an essay writer says what they are going to say, says it, then says it again. This really is a circular, rather than a linear way of writing.
>
> (Pennycook, personal communication)

Other times, a writing advisor may look at a student's family name and make assumptions about their writing on the basis of this, without knowing if they are indeed of that language and culture background. An example of this is an Australian student with a Chinese husband who was given advice on the circular nature of 'oriental' writing and the need to be more western in her writing on the basis of her (Chinese) family name. In this case, the advisor pre-judged the student's writing and made assumptions about it solely on his preconceived ideas about Chinese and English academic writing and the student's ethnicity (Pennycook 2001).

An important feature of a well-written text is the unity and connectedness with which individual sentences relate to each other. This is, in part, the result of how ideas are presented in the text, but also depends on the ways in which the writer has created cohesive links within and between sentences as well as within and between paragraphs in the text. This is especially important for English writing which is sometimes referred to as *writer-responsible,* as opposed to other languages (such as Japanese) where written texts are sometimes described as being *reader-responsible* (see Chapter 3 for further discussion of this). That is, in English it is often the writer's responsibility to make the sense of their text clear to their reader. Theses and dissertations in English, then, are characterized by a large amount of 'display of knowledge'; that is, telling the reader something they may already know and, in some cases, may know better than the student. Often a second-language student will say 'I didn't say that because I thought you already knew it'. This, however, is exactly what thesis and dissertation writers do in English, and is something many second-language students may find strange or unnatural.

It is important, then, not to take a stereotyped view of how students from one culture will necessarily write in another. There may be substantial differences, and there may not. It is not always easy to predict what these differences may be. One way of finding this out is to ask students if they have written the same kind of text in their first language and in what ways that text was similar or different to the one they are now writing in English. Prince (2000) did this in a study in which she asked Polish and Chinese students who had already written a dissertation in their first language how similar or different they found dissertation writing in English. She found that, although the students had all written a dissertation in their first language, they had little idea of how they should do this in English. She also found that different students had different views on how they wanted to represent themselves in their English texts. She argues that we 'should be wary of generalizing about students from different cultural backgrounds, because all students are individuals' (Prince 2000: 1) and may have their own preferences and ways of writing that are especially important to them.

Speaking across cultures

There is also potential for misunderstandings between students and their supervisors in the kind of cross-cultural setting involved in supervising a second-language student. The area of research known as *cross-cultural pragmatics* looks at this in particular. Researchers in this area have looked at the difficulties created by transferring one behaviour or rhetorical strategy into another language and culture without realizing things may be done differently in that language and culture. It may be something as simple as walking into someone's office without knocking (because they saw the door was open) or it may involve transferring the way of asking for something from one culture into another without realizing the way of doing this is different in the other language and culture. A student may think, for example, that adding the word 'please' adds politeness to a request, which in some ways it does, without realizing that sending their supervisor an email saying 'I've finished Chapter 3. Please check it' is not sufficiently polite (in most circumstances) for this kind of request.

Different views of cultural appropriateness, thus, can lead to misunderstandings and prevent effective cross-cultural communication. This is particularly the case where students and supervisors come from different language and cultural backgrounds. As Cargill (2000) points out, although students have passed the university's English language admission requirements, they are often under-prepared for the face-to-face interactions that are part of the student/supervisor arrangement. These face-to-face interactions are a crucial part of the supervisory process. They are, however, fraught with the potential for misunderstandings, especially in cross-cultural communication situations (Moses 1984).

Supervisors and students, then, need to be aware of and expect cross-cultural differences in their interactions with each other. If communication problems arise, they need to be prepared to talk about them. Native speakers of a language, in fact, are often much less tolerant of these kinds of errors in cross-cultural communication situations than they are, for example, of grammatical errors. If a student says something the supervisor thought was rude, it is easy for the supervisor to think the student 'meant to be rude', rather than that they did not now how to do something in a culturally different way. These are issues which are discussed in further chapters of the book.

Applications

1 Ask your student to tell you what is typical of academic writing in their first language and culture. Then ask them to compare this to their understanding of academic writing in English.
2 Ask your student to think of a situation where they have had a cross-cultural communication problem in an academic setting. Discuss what happened and what might have caused the miscommunication. Think of ways in which the situation might have been resolved.

Second-language academic writing and identity

Writer identity is a key issue in written academic discourse, and especially thesis and dissertation writing. This is a particularly difficult issue for many second-language writers. Academic writing is often presented to students as something that is faceless and impersonal. Students are told, for example, 'to leave their personalities at the door' (Hyland 2002: 352) and not to use personal pronouns such as 'I' which show what is being said is the student's view or place in things. As Hyland points out, however, 'almost everything we write says something about us and the sort of relationship that we want to set up with our readers'. Establishing writer identity is often difficult for second-language writers. This is further complicated by students having a different way of writing and different 'voice' in their first-language academic writing (see Hirvela and Belcher 2001 for further discussion of this).

Prince (2000) looked at the issue of writer identity in second-language thesis writing. Her interest was in the ways in which second-language writers might be influenced (or not) by their experience of having written a thesis in their first language and culture. She looked at the experiences of a group of Chinese and Polish students, all of whom had written a thesis in their first language prior to writing a thesis in English. She found a major theme that emerged in her study was whether the students had to give up, or change, their personal identity in order to write a successful thesis in English. Prince tells how one of her Polish students, Ilona, fiercely fought to retain her personal and individual style of writing, but in the end found she had to give this away in order to pass.

Bartolome (1998: xiii) argues that learning to succeed in western academic settings is not just a matter of language, but of knowing the 'linguistically contextualised language' of the particular discourse that is valued in the particular academic setting. Many students find this a difficult thing to do. They may fear a loss of cultural identity and not wish to be 'drowned' in the new academic culture. Ilona, the Polish student in Prince's study, felt exactly this. Other student experiences reported on in the research literature, however, have been slightly different. A Chinese student, for example, in Shen's (1989) study felt that learning to write in a new way added another dimension to himself and to his view of the world. This did not mean, he said, that he had lost his Chinese identity. Indeed, he said, he would never lose this. Students do, however, have to learn to write in a way that is often new and different for them and have to balance their new identity with their old one. This is as much about cultural views of writing as it is about new and different relationships between student writers with their new and imagined readers, their supervisors and their examiners. As Silva and Matsuda point out, writing is always embedded in a complex web of relationships between writers and readers. These relationships, further, are constantly changing. As they argue:

> the writer's task is not as simple as constructing an accurate representation of reality; the writer also has to negotiate, through the construction of the text, his or her own view of these elements of writing with the views held by the readers.
>
> (Silva and Matsuda 2002: 253)

Student writers, then:

> do not write in isolation but within networks of more and less powerfully situated colleagues and community members. They learn to forge alliances with those community members with whom they share values or whom they perceive will benefit them in some way and to resist when accommodating does not suit them.
>
> (Casanave 2002: xiii–xiv)

These are all factors that influence what a student writes and how they position themselves in relation to what they write.

A further complication is that some students may come from backgrounds where they have considerable standing in their field of study and find it difficult to be told they need to take on the voice of a novice academic writer as they write in their second language. Hirvela and Belcher (2001) discuss this issue, arguing that we need to know more about the ways our students present themselves in their first-language writing, and about their first-language and culture identities, so we can help them deal with the issue of identity in their second-language academic writing. The issue of writer identity, thus, is important and is a theme we return to in later chapters of this book.

Applications

1   Ask your student to discuss how they show their opinion about something in their first-language writing. Is this the same in English or different? How easy or difficult do they find doing this in English? Why?

2   The quotes below relate what some second-language students in a study carried out by Cadman (2000) had to say about expressing opinions in thesis writing. Show these to your student and ask them to comment on them. How similar or different are these to how they feel?

It's not really easy to be critical of the works of others. This is contrary to what I've learned from my mother who was my first teacher.

To criticize and to judge the articles or literature are something new for me, because in my undergraduate study in [my home country] our study approaches were more passive, we became receivers of knowledge and we rarely argued about our subjects.

Disciplinary differences in thesis and dissertation writing

Disciplinary differences in academic writing have been studied by a number of researchers. Ken Hyland (1999; 2005; 2005b) for example has looked at disciplinary differences in research articles and academic textbooks. These are not the same as theses and dissertations, however. Research articles and textbooks have different audiences and different goals from theses and dissertations. Research articles, as mentioned earlier, are 'experts writing for experts'. Thesis and dissertation writing, however, is much more a case of students writing 'for admission to an area of study'. While there are some similarities between each of these kinds of texts, there are also important differences.

Hyland's (2004a) study of master's and doctoral students' writing points to many of the unique features of thesis and dissertation writing, as well as important disciplinary differences in this kind of writing. One important feature he examines is *metadiscourse* in thesis and dissertation writing; that is, the ways thesis writers use language to organize what they want to say in their text, how they 'shape their arguments to the needs and expectations of their target readers' (Hyland 2004a: 134) and how they show their stance towards the content and the reader of their text. This topic is returned to in detail later in this book. It is important to point out, however, that Hyland did find there were important differences in the use of metadiscourse across disciplines. He also found there were differences in the use of metadiscourse across degrees. He found, for example, that PhD students used much more metadiscourse to show the organization of their texts than did master's students. This could be partly explained, he suggests, by the longer length of PhD texts requiring students to show the arrangement of their texts more than at the master's level. It could also be, he suggests, the result of doctoral students being generally more sophisticated writers than master's students and much more aware of the need to write reader-friendly texts and to engage with their readers. In terms of disciplinary differences he found social science disciplines used the most metadiscourse overall, especially in the use of hedges (such as *possible, might, tend to* and *perhaps*). The social sciences students also used more attitude markers (such as *unfortunately, surprisingly,* and *interestingly*) and self mentions (such as *I, we, my* and *our*).

Thompson (1999) carried out a study in which he interviewed PhD supervisors about organization, presentation, citation and argumentation practices in PhD theses in different areas of study. He looked, in particular, at theses written in the areas of agricultural botany and agricultural economics. He found a wide range of differences, even in the length of the texts that he examined. He also found quite different views of how students were told they should position themselves in relation to their texts. One supervisor, for example, argued that the research project should be the main focus of the thesis and the author should not intrude on this by using the personal 'I' in their writing. Another supervisor gave the opposite advice when he felt the use of personal pronouns would help the student to communicate their ideas. Thompson's work suggests that is really not possible to say there is one single way in which theses and dissertations should be written in a university. How the thesis is written will be influenced by a number of things. It will be influenced by the set of values underlying the particular discipline in which it is written, by the research perspective the student adopts, as well as by advice that is given to the student by their supervisor (see Chapter 5 for further discussion of thesis types and disciplinary differences in thesis and dissertation writing).

Applications

1   The chart in Figure 1.1 illustrates the relationship between the student's text, their course of study, the academic discipline in which they are writing, and the institution in which they are studying. Each of these has an influence on the form and content of the students' text and needs to be considered in terms of its influence on what students write and how they write it. Ask your student to look at this figure and to discuss how each of these impact on what they write and how they write it.

2   Ask your student to go to the library, or to search an online thesis database (see Chapter 12), and make a copy of the table of contents of three theses or dissertations written in their area of study. Ask them also to copy the table of contents from three theses or dissertations written in other, quite different, areas of study. Ask your student to make notes about the similarities and differences between each of these theses or dissertations. What seems to be typical of a thesis or dissertation written in their area of study and what does not?

What universities and examiners expect of theses and dissertations

While theses and dissertations may be written differently in different areas of study, universities typically apply the same criteria to their examination. Many universities send examiners a list of criteria to refer to while they are reading a student's thesis or dissertation. These often vary according to the level of study. They are normally, however, some kind of variation on the following list of points:

- an awareness and understanding of relevant previous research on the topic;
- a critical appraisal of previous research on the topic;
- a clearly defined and comprehensive investigation of the topic;
- the appropriate application of research methods and techniques;
- a thorough presentation and interpretation of results;

- appropriately developed conclusions and implications that are linked to the research framework and findings;
- a high standard of literary quality and presentation;
- a contribution to knowledge on the particular topic.

The last of these points, contribution to knowledge, is especially important at the PhD level where examiners are often asked if the thesis 'makes a substantive original contribution' to knowledge in the particular area. It is helpful to discuss these criteria with students early on in their candidature so they can consider how they impact on how they carry out and write up their research.

A special edition of the *International Journal of Educational Research* published in 2004 addressed the issue of doctoral thesis examination. The study by Holbrook *et al.* (2004) published in this issue looked at 803 examiners' reports on 301 theses from three different universities. From their analysis they identified the list of qualities shown in Table 1.3 (on p.19) as being characteristic of 'high quality' PhD theses. Their definition of a high quality thesis was one that was accepted for the degree by all examiners without requiring any revisions. These qualities include the significance of the student's research topic, potential of the thesis for publication, use of the research literature in the design of the study and writing of the thesis, logic

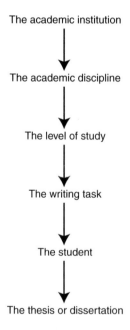

Figure 1.1 Text and context in academic writing
Source: adapted from Samraj 2002

Table 1.3 Characteristics of high and low quality theses

General criteria	Specific criteria	
	High quality theses	*Low quality theses*
Thesis topic and approach	Significance and challenge of the topic Fusion of originality of the approach with realization of a significant contribution to the field	Questionable integrity of the approach of thesis or presentation of findings
Literature review	Expert use of the literature in design of the study and discussion of the findings Thorough, clear and incisive reporting of the literature	Inadequate coverage or focus of the literature in relation to the study Inaccuracies and omissions in referencing
Communicative competence		Manifest editorial inadequacies
Publications arising	Recognized need for early publication of/from the study	

Source: Holbrook *et al.* 2004: 117

and clarity of the reporting and discussion of findings, and the extent to which the findings can be applied in the field.

Holbrook and her colleagues also identified characteristics of 'low quality' PhD theses. Low quality theses were defined as theses that were required to be revised and resubmitted for re-examination by at least half of the examiners. The characteristics of these theses are also shown in Table 1.3. With low quality theses there was a wider range of agreement amongst examiners. The reports written for these theses were much longer than those that were written for high quality theses. They contained a preponderance of instructed comment, more negative judgment, and a greater emphasis on editorial errors and inaccuracies in the referencing of the literature than was the case for high quality thesis reports.

Applications

1   Ask your student to look at the criteria on pp.17–18 and in Table 1.3 and discuss how each of these impacts on how they will carry out and write up their research.
2   The following are quotes from studies which have looked at thesis examination. Ask your student to read these quotes and to discuss what they mean for the writing of their thesis.

A research thesis ought to:

- be a report of work that others would want to read;
- tell a compelling story articulately whilst pre-empting inevitable critiques;
- carry the reader into complex realms, and inform and educate him/her;
- be sufficiently speculative or original to command respectful peer attention.

  (Winter *et al.* 2000: 32–35; Mullins and Kiley 2002: 372)

One of the common descriptors of a poor thesis, across all disciplines, was 'sloppiness'. Sloppiness might be demonstrated by typographical errors, or mistakes in calculations, referencing or footnotes. The concern with sloppiness was that examiners considered it was an indication that the research itself might not be rigorous and the results and conclusions could not be trusted.

  (Mullins and Kiley 2002: 378)

Overview of the book

This chapter has provided a background to thesis and dissertation writing as well as introducing a number of issues that are of particular relevance to second-language thesis and dissertation writers. It has discussed the social and cultural contexts of thesis and dissertation writing and factors within this context that impact on the writing of the student's thesis and dissertation. It has discussed the relationship between thesis writers and readers, including what examiners expect to see in a successful student text. It has also discussed disciplinary differences in thesis and dissertation writing, as well as approaches to knowledge at different levels of study. Cross-cultural issues and writer identity in thesis and dissertation writing have also been discussed. A number of these themes will be taken up in greater detail further in the book.

The next chapter of the book discusses what it means to be a non-native-speaker research student in an English-medium university. It looks at definitions of the 'non-native-speaker student' and the challenges that face non-native-speaker students in this role. It discusses, in more detail, cross-cultural communication problems between non-native-speaker students and their supervisors as well as suggesting strategies for dealing with these. It also offers suggestions for ways in which supervisors can help support non-native-speaker students in learning to become successful research students and thesis or dissertation writers.

Note

1 The terms 'thesis' and 'dissertation' are used in different ways in different parts of the world. In this book, the term 'dissertation' is used for undergraduate and master's degrees and 'thesis' for doctoral degrees.

Chapter 2

Working with second-language speakers of English

> The first language of many international candidates is not English and this adds to the time and effort supervisors in all disciplines put into verbal communication and candidates' written work. Supervisors are additionally burdened both by their knowledge of the distinct linguistic, cultural, familial and professional pressures that international candidates' circumstances exert on the candidate, and by perceived financial pressures from universities to take on increasing numbers of full-fee-paying international candidates.
>
> (Sinclair 2005: 19)

Introduction

The above extract from a recent investigation into the pedagogy of 'good' PhD supervision provides a summary of the motivation behind the writing of this book. Supervising research students who are second-language speakers of English, whatever the language background of the supervisor, provides an additional challenge in terms of the multiple factors alluded to in the quote. It would appear that there is an absence of relevant material in this area that might support supervisors of second-language speakers. A recent survey of 22 guides to supervising doctoral students and dissertation writing revealed that only five of the books provided a comprehensive analysis of the needs of international students (Dedrick and Watson 2002).

At the same time, it is our experience that many international students, regardless of language background, are uniquely placed to carry out and contribute to important and valuable research by virtue of the diverse perspectives that they are able to bring to the research. Not all second-language speakers of English enrolled in research degrees are however international students: many are citizens or permanent residents of the country in which they are studying and the topic begs a wider investigation. Above all, our intention in writing this book is to reduce the perception that the supervision of students from non-English-speaking backgrounds need be an 'additional burden'.

Second-language research students in the era of globalization

The issue of who second-language English-speaking students are is a vexed one linguistically, educationally and politically. We acknowledge that being a speaker of English as a second, third or fourth language is very much a feature of the globalized reality of the twenty-first century and that, for many, the dominance of English at the perceived expense of other languages is not unproblematic.

In 1999, Graddol estimated that the overall number of native speakers of English as a percentage of the world's population was declining. Depending on the criteria used to define non-nativeness, native English speakers may already constitute a minority. Moreover, as Swales (2004) points out, the internationalization and the concomitant Anglicization of the research world have encouraged the dominance of English as the international language of research. The clear divisions of say 20 or 30 years ago, characterized by academics who were predominantly English first-language speakers supervising the research of growing numbers of second-language students, have given way to today's more complex picture. Many supervisors would themselves be from a non-English-speaking background and would be publishing and communicating in English via conferences, journals and books. Moreover, there are thousands of second-language graduate students engaged in master's and doctoral studies in countries such as Hong Kong, Singapore and in other parts of Asia and indeed in Africa, where English is essential for reading and writing but not necessarily used in daily communication with supervisors and colleagues (Braine 2002). Rather than a dichotomy between first- and second-language speakers of English, it may be more useful, Swales suggests, to think of academic English proficiency as a continuum. At one pole are broadly English proficient (BEP) scholars and researchers who are either first- or second-language speakers of English and, if second-language speakers, practically academically bilingual within their disciplinary field, and, at the other pole, those scholars who are more narrowly English proficient (NEP). NEP researchers are second-language speakers who may be commencing advanced study in an anglophone country and may have only a reading knowledge of academic English and weaker oral or written abilities. They are often, but not always, what Swales refers to as junior researchers: those starting out on their academic or other careers including PhD candidates, postdoctoral scholars and new researchers, while senior researchers are academics well established in the anglophone world of research, writing and publication.

We have tried to capture these interrelationships in a simple matrix (see Figure 2.1). It is only the BEP senior researcher who requires little or no assistance with successful research communication. Junior researchers, whether first- or second-language speakers, can all benefit from more explicit research communication induction, while the NEP senior researcher may still be

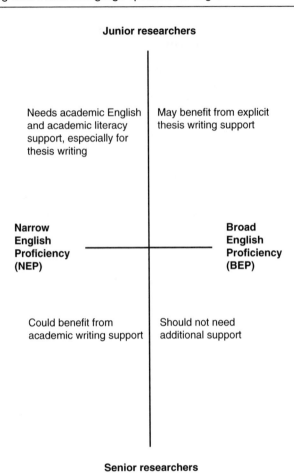

Junior researchers

Needs academic English and academic literacy support, especially for thesis writing

May benefit from explicit thesis writing support

Narrow English Proficiency (NEP)

Broad English Proficiency (BEP)

Could benefit from academic writing support

Should not need additional support

Senior researchers

Figure 2.1 Interrelationships between level of English language proficiency and research status

struggling with publication and communication in English. The growing number of journal articles and handbooks on the topic of assisting academics with writing for publication bear testimony to the notion of academic writing development as being on a continuum (e.g. Grant and Knowles 2000; Lee and Boud 2003; Morss and Murray 2001; Murray 2004).

The groups that our book is primarily designed to assist are the junior researchers who fall into the NEP category and those who are supervising their dissertation writing. To quote Swales again:

> NEP individuals are typically those who are identified as needing further EAP [English for Academic Purposes] help when they undertake Anglophone or largely Anglophone advanced degrees [...]. These groups

typically have greater difficulty in establishing an academic identity in an era when English (however unfortunately) has come to occupy an increasingly dominating position.

(Swales 2004: 57)

We believe that supervisors of junior researchers who are located further towards the BEP end of the continuum may also find the book helpful. Our own experience of working with a wide range of research students has shown us that the majority of students will benefit from a more explicit induction into research writing.

For all students, writing a thesis is a challenge; for those writing in English whose first language is not English, the challenges are even greater. However, as a second-language PhD student of Cadman's (1997: 11) concluded, 'cross-cultural differences are a matter of degree not kind'.

Whereas 20 to 30 years ago the issue for 'western' universities was how second-language students, particularly international students, would adjust or acculturate to the 'host' English-speaking country, there is now a growing recognition that they are part of the global movement of people whose identities, perhaps through the very fact of sojourning elsewhere to study and work, are less linked to a specific community and more to cultural globalization (Bradley 2000: 419). Becoming 'more Western' is certainly not the desired outcome (Kiley 2003: 354). However, some students will feel more easily 'at home' in the new academic community than others for whom the 'costs' involved are substantial – not solely in financial terms but in terms of the struggle to cope successfully in an environment which presents linguistic, educational and cultural challenges (Banerjee 2003). Surviving and writing a thesis in a 'foreign' environment in a second or third language may take its toll on student and supervisor. Supervisors, for example, consistently indicate that they spend more time assisting second-language students with drafting their work (Sinclair 2005).

In the next section, we consider some of the potential 'costs' that the second-language student may bear and, in the section that follows, we discuss ways in which supervisors may attempt to minimize these costs to the student and their impact on the student–supervisor relationship. Not all the issues that affect second-language speakers can be resolved at the student–supervisor level, however. We are fully aware that institutions and overly enthusiastic recruiters may unduly raise student expectations of what is available to them in terms of resources and achievable in terms of their language proficiency. The high fees that international students pay may also create a climate of expectation that can impact on the student–supervisor relationship. The individual supervisor should always look to departmental colleagues and to the institution for support as it appears to be the case that support initiatives are increasing (see Chapter 12 for a list of additional resources that may help supervisors).

'I just say yes all the time but I am not happy. In my head I feel like a fool': exploring 'cost'

Mei, a PhD student from China whose words are cited above (Aspland 1999: 29), struggled with what she perceived as her original supervisor's lack of expertise in her area and an absence of structure and explicit direction. Although unhappy, she felt unable to question his authority:

> I can judge now that he had no specialized knowledge of my topic, but we Chinese are humble and do not like to question these matters. I continued to assume that he must be the best person because of the recommendation by the authorities.
>
> (Aspland 1999: 29)

She felt it would be a sign of disrespect to articulate her unhappiness:

> I am very embarrassed because things with this supervisor are not right. [...] I am too frightened to challenge him or the authorities. I just say yes all the time but I am not happy. In my head I feel like a fool.
>
> (Aspland 1999: 29)

Mei later changed supervisors and had an extremely positive experience that will be referred to later when we examine the characteristics of successful supervision of second-language students. The costs to Mei in terms of this unhappy experience were not merely financial, although she struggled to support herself without a scholarship, but also substantial in terms of damage to her self-esteem and confidence in her abilities.

Cadman (2005) has pointed out that some international research students entering western research contexts for the first time may experience difficulty with the absence of set topics or prescribed reading lists and few set tasks other than the research proposal. This absence illustrates the not always explicit expectation that research students should take responsibility for directing their own learning, that autonomy is required and that students must self-manage their writing. Supervisors need to be mindful of cross-cultural miscommunication that may arise through such differing sets of expectations, and how these may lead to stereotypical views of their students and, in turn, to students not developing more confident, peer-like relationships with their supervisors.

Challenges of the new student role

As indicated in the previous section, second-language thesis writers are by no means a homogenous group (Bradley 2000). They may be residents or citizens of the country in which they are studying but speak English as a second or third language. They can be young PhD or master's students about to launch an academic career, established academics in their country of origin, or perhaps scholarship holders or professionals in their own countries who are on leave from employment in government or non-government agencies. They may have previously studied in an English-medium environment or they may have left home for the first time. They may be accompanied by spouses and children or they may be alone (Cadman 2005). International students in western universities tend to be older, married and well established in their professional careers prior to commencing postgraduate study. The decision to enrol in a research degree can be seen as an investment by the candidate. International second-language students may feel under intense pressure to succeed as they are scholarship holders or have jobs to return to. Other challenges identified in the literature that will be familiar to many supervisors include finances, family support (both back home or in the host country), friendships, isolation, loss of social status and the hidden rules that govern interactions (Bradley 2000; Myles and Cheng 2003).

In their study of postgraduate students at a British university, Humphrey and McCarthy (1999) found that international postgraduate students who spoke English as a second language were more likely to be older, married and better established in their careers than the local students who tended to be recent graduates, young and single. International students could, therefore, benefit from additional support in their transition to the student role. According to Humphrey and McCarthy, international postgraduates from certain countries may expect the university to take a more protective role towards their students than tends to be the case in British universities. A 34-year-old male PhD student from South Korea stated: 'In my country students are the university's moral responsibility' (cited in Humphrey and McCarthy 1999: 385). Students may expect the university to provide accommodation and be shocked when this is not the case:

> [The University] accepts no responsibility for overseas students. It is completely different from our country. For example, in my own country there were some undergraduate students from other countries, from some Arab countries and the government felt very much a responsibility about them because they believe they are our guests.
>
> (28-year-old male Iranian PhD student
> cited in Humphrey and McCarthy 1999: 385)

International second-language postgraduate students are often members of the elite in their home countries – accustomed to enjoying high status and shouldering responsibility – so becoming a student can lead to a 'temporary lowering of status and power' (Humphrey and McCarthy 1999: 384). Some of the students interviewed by Humphrey and McCarthy felt strongly that their difference from the local students was not being acknowledged: 'Most of the postgraduate students, especially from overseas, are not recognized at all. We are treated just like students, forgetting that some of us are also lecturing in the universities in our various countries' (36-year-old male Nigerian PhD student); and 'We should be involved in the Department activity and treated like junior staff' (36-year-old male Malaysian PhD student) (both cited in Humphrey and McCarthy 1999: 384).

The spouses of international students may also have to adapt to quite different circumstances, together with loss of identity and status. Families and children will also need different types of accommodation from individual students and inappropriate housing is often a source of cost and stress to the students. The following quotes from international students in the UK reveal the impact the non-academic factors highlighted above can have on the postgraduate student experience:

> 'People do not understand my background ... they do not understand where I am coming from when I make a point or a comment' (PhD student of military background, funded by military).
>
> 'Both used to comfort ... here ... my wife is scared to go out ... house problems do interfere with my work'.
>
> 'I have not seen my husband for 7 months ... this week I am extremely happy as he is coming next Friday – I can't wait for that day – our separation affects my work'.
>
> '... here suddenly I was put in a very small room, not very clean and I had to share the bathroom, the toilet and kitchen with other people – this was very depressing ... in one year I had to move five times'.
>
> 'If they weren't in school I probably would find it very difficult here in England ... it is always a struggle ... bring them to school, collect them, make dinner, prepare lunch, give time to them, read to them'.
>
> 'English people are not easy to make friends with'.
>
> 'I do not spend much time on the campus, I come in specifically to see the seminars, to see my supervisors ... I rarely share my experiences with other students ... I used to meet them more during the methods course, sometimes a little before or sometimes a little after the sessions ... Sometimes I meet one or another of them in the corridor and ask "how are you getting on" but it is superficial'.
>
> (Deem and Brehony 2000: 154–155)

Student poverty may compound a lack of access to decent housing and other facilities, especially in the case of students from less wealthy countries who are often less well funded or may have fewer additional resources on which to draw. Postgraduate students from countries outside of Europe who were surveyed by Humphrey and McCarthy (1999) in Newcastle upon Tyne were

more likely to live in the city's poorest neighbourhood with the greatest
social problems and poor housing stock as the rents were more affordable.
This potential disadvantage was offset by the better-represented groups having well-organized support structures. However, as indicated by the students
cited below, less well-off students may be struggling to afford photocopying
or postage stamps for survey mailouts or be unsure as to whether they may use
the departmental fax machine and phones, yet be reluctant to raise these matters with their supervisor for fear of crossing an invisible boundary.

'I think one of the major problems here is about the facilities that are
offered to us. I'm not talking about computers or printers ... I'm talking
about simple things like photocopying. I'm sure a lot of people go and
get cards from the departments, but this is not for every student.'

'I'm not sure the things I can use ... I do think that things should be
included ... even postage stamps ... Because you are sending out questionnaires. Because you are paying quite a lot, especially if you are an
overseas student, and you don't see your supervisor that much.'

'Even now, after 2 years here, I don't know if I can use the telephone in
the department.'

(cited in Deem and Brehony 2000: 159)

Cross-cultural communication:
differing expectations

As Mei's story illustrated, differing expectations of the student/supervisor
roles and different communication styles can cause the relationship to
founder. Students and supervisors will both have expectations about the
process and relationships but because many of these expectations are implicit
and based on a notion of trust there is always a risk that they will deteriorate
if the implicit expectations of one partner are not reciprocated (Kiley 1998).
Successful cross-cultural communication requires intensive negotiation and
collaboration (Adams and Cargill 2003).

Hockey (1996) argues that most supervisor–student relationships in the
British context take the form of 'comradeship' – based on personal trust and
characterized by a relaxed interactional style, the use of first names by both
parties and with agreements as to timeframes and schedules being made
orally and with little explicit negotiation of expectations of mutual responsibilities. The second-language student may come from an educational setting
in which such informal relationships are most unusual and quite disconcerting. Uncertainty over the levels of formality in face-to-face interactions is
often mentioned by second-language international students. The 'rules' gov-
erning these are often not easily discernible to outsiders. In many western,
anglophone university settings, students and supervisors are regularly on

first-name terms which may, as Myles and Cheng (2003) point out, be unsettling for students used to much more formal, distant relationships between student and professor. They may also mistake informality for friendship and not be aware of invisible boundaries circumscribing the relationship. An Indian student studying in Canada commented:

> Culture is different. We respect teachers a lot in my culture ... at first I felt so confused. I just don't feel good to call them David or ... I don't feel good to call them by their first names ... . You need to think every time which term I need to call them.
>
> (cited in Myles and Cheng 2003: 253)

It may be that the student comes from a different 'politeness system' – one that relies more on demonstrating deference to a socially defined 'superior', whereas the supervisor, although perhaps only superficially so, is ambivalent towards such a system and wishes to appear more egalitarian (Cargill 1998). The issue of the use of the first name versus the academic title may be a surface manifestation of a more fundamental mismatch in communication styles, to which the supervisor needs to be sensitive. In cross-linguistic and cross-cultural supervisory conversations, supervisors should, for example, be aware that pauses may have different meaning. In English, a longish pause may indicate that the other partner (the student) may now introduce a new topic. The student may, however, be from a culture in which the person with higher social status has the right to introduce the new topic so the student's silence may be interpreted as the student having nothing to say, while the student is in fact waiting for the supervisor to speak. If this is a persistent pattern, the supervisor may be tempted to 'fill in the gaps' and the student may come to be seen as linguistically less able than they may in fact be. For instance, Mei's perception of this mismatch of communication patterns was that her supervisor expected that she 'interrupt all the time and not worry about being rude. He wanted me to be more like the Australian students' (Aspland 1999: 31).

As Kiley (1998) points out, differing expectations may affect students' ability to approach their supervisor. Indonesian postgraduate students in Australia, for example, may believe that it is the supervisor who needs to take the initiative in calling a meeting, whereas Australian supervisors often feel that it is up to the student to contact the supervisor if they have a problem and will assume that if they don't hear from the student then all is going well. She quotes 'Watie', an Indonesian student who commented: 'A supervisor should be understanding about the culture. Like here, if you don't ask anything then it means that everything is OK, but in Indonesia it means that everything is wrong' (Kiley 1998: 197).

Dong (1998: 379) identified a similar potential for a mismatch in expectations among the second-language graduate students she surveyed:

'if he [my advisor] can read and correct or even rephrase the whole thing, I will learn how the same thing could have been communicated in a rather effective manner' (Urdu speaker).

'I want my advisor to provide me with the newest research development and materials concerning my topics' (Korean speaker).

'just be more interested [in what I am doing]' (German speaker).

'[my advisor] make me aware of the requirements of the school' (Tamil speaker).

Similarly, in a laboratory situation, simply asking 'do you understand the problem?' may elicit 'yes' for an answer from second-language students experiencing difficulty with an experiment, but may be masking a lack of confidence or a feeling that asking for help is an expression of failure. Supervisors need to observe the student closely and to provide more explicit guidance and direction as well as trying to develop a relationship in which the student will feel more comfortable expressing uncertainty. Directing the student to other more established students in the laboratory may also help the student build support networks (Frost 1999: 106).

In addition, students may have good written academic English skills but be less fluent in face-to-face oral communication or more colloquial English. Myles and Cheng (2003) cite the example of an international second-language student who felt her supervisor was critical of her English ability because she struggled with the more colloquial language needed to draft a questionnaire. Students with high entry-level test scores may still experience major difficulties with everyday interactions, both socially and academically, as well as with intercultural adjustment (Dong 1997). Similarly, students may also have difficulty communicating about emotional or personal matters directly affecting their study as they may not have the resources in English to express feelings that are tied to their first language or they may feel uncomfortable talking to someone from a different cultural background and/or gender (Bradley 2000). Yuriko Nagata, a Japanese woman who completed graduate studies in the US and Australia, commented on her early experience of studying in another language: 'I used to suffer from my own double perception of myself – the mature socially functioning person in my native language and the incompetent non-communicator in the target language' (Nagata 1999: 18).

An Australian study (Geake and Maingard 1999) found that whereas for supervisors, language- and writing-related problems were seen as highly significant, the second-language students believed that, having been admitted to the university, their language was appropriate for academic study. Supervisors should also be aware that studies of advanced language learners in academic settings consistently indicate that scientific vocabulary acquisition remains a difficulty for second-language speakers, even those who are relatively highly proficient in English (Banerjee 2003; Shaw 1991). Students may be familiar with terms in a written context but may also be unfamiliar with these terms in spoken English (i.e. when pronounced) and may not immediately understand what the supervisor is referring to. Politeness strategies may impinge on the students' ability to ask for clarification as they may not wish to appear not to know the meaning of a term.

Supervisors should be aware that the use of indirect suggestions (e.g. 'perhaps you might want to look at X': a politeness strategy that suggests equality) may create the impression that the student has the option not to follow up on the suggestion when, in fact, the existence of the power relationship means that the student does not have an option. Similarly, students, when making suggestions, may be so tentative (not wanting to appear lacking in deference) that they may run the risk of appearing to lack drive and initiative (Cargill 1998).

Second-language students may expect their supervisors to demonstrate a sensitivity to cultural diversity. Myles and Cheng cite a Taiwanese student studying in Canada who was critical of what she perceived to be a professor's limited awareness:

> Like if you want to teach, you need to know your students, right. And nowadays your students come from all over the world so should all the content they teach. [...] Do they point out their cultural bias or do they point out their conceptual baggage? [...] Like one Prof., it's a joke among international students here and he says, 'I went to the conference. We have planners from all over the world, Los Angeles, Vancouver, Toronto, Chicago, New York.' Actually all the cities he mentioned are U.S. and Canada. That's all over the world to them already.
>
> (Myles and Cheng 2003: 252)

Access to research culture and social networks

Several studies (e.g. Casanave 1995; Deem and Brehony 2000; Dong 1998) suggest that second-language and international students' access to the academic research culture of their field of study, to student peer culture and to research training is generally not equal to that of local, native-English-speaking students, despite the students' strong desire to access these. Academic research cultures include disciplinary or interdisciplinary ideas and values, particular kinds of expert knowledge and knowledge production, cultural practices and narratives, departmental sociability and intellectual networks (Deem and Brehony 2000). Student access to these cultures and to research training appears to depend, particularly in the social sciences and humanities, on 'chance and supervisors' (Deem and Brehony 2000: 158). Much of the knowledge of these practices is tacitly known to those who are successful 'insiders' and is therefore not easily articulated by supervisors to newcomers. Social sciences and humanities students moreover lack the team-based environments and the opportunities for *ad hoc* interactions with the supervisor and colleagues which the sciences and engineering provide. It appears that second-language speakers may be less able to access the informal learning opportunities which are important for postgraduate socialization. Deem and Brehony (2000) found that international students mentioned informal academic networks and encouragement to attend seminars and conferences much less often than did local students and concluded that implicit exclusion may be marginalizing international and second-language students. Sung (2000) identified a cluster of factors as contributing to the 'rounded socioacademic success' of a group of Taiwanese doctoral students. These included relationships with supervisors and fellow students as well as an active role in presentations and in departmental activities and social events.

Dong's (1998) survey of over 100 first- and second-language students writing their master's or doctoral dissertation at two large US research universities revealed that social isolation was more of an issue for the second-language speakers than for their native speaker peers, despite the students typically working in a team or laboratory environment. Just over half of the second-language students stated that they talked to staff and other students about their theses/dissertations either infrequently or had not yet done so as compared with only 37 per cent of the native English speakers who had a similar response. Nearly half of the second-language writers reported having no help with their writing other than from their supervisor, although many expressed a desire for native speaker help with their writing. Close to one in five of the second-language students stated they had no interaction with their peers or other staff at all in regard to their writing. Dong found that the students tended to rely on students from their home countries for assistance and generally demonstrated little uptake of available resources. She concluded that a lack of social networks disadvantaged second-language students in terms of access to helpful resources and development opportunities such as publication and that the lack might be due to the poor communication skills of the second-language speakers as well as to native speakers' reluctance to interact with non-native speakers, possibly because of perceived communication difficulties.

Sung (2000) found that the English language proficiency of the Taiwanese doctoral students she studied most directly influenced their academic performance in terms of being able to secure teaching or research positions, and also affected their interactions with their advisors and peers. Students' willingness to improve their English was a factor in their academic success. Those who cited time and workload pressure as the reason for not pursuing English support were often the students who most needed to work on their language and their poor language was hindering their progress.

Dai's story outlined in Box 2.1 (on p.34) highlights the vicious circle that the challenges of being a second-language student in an unfamiliar context can lead to.

Box 2.1 Dai's story

Dai was a student from China in her late thirties who enrolled for a PhD at an Australian university. Her spoken and written English was poor and she also had little prior knowledge of the new area to which she was moving. In her supervisor's view she was effectively learning two languages – that of the new disciplinary area and academic English. Despite attending numerous writing courses and working very hard, she made very slow progress and her supervisor became extremely concerned. Making Dai's life harder was the fact that she had left her husband and young daughter in China and there was little likelihood that they would join her. Dai was socially isolated partly due to her poor language skills but also due to her total immersion in her study which was in part due to her poor language skills but also to the conceptual gaps. After a year, she returned home. She was awarded a Graduate Diploma, allowing her to salvage something from the situation. It later emerged that Dai had not met the university's English language requirements but a well-intentioned member of the faculty had exercised his right to admit her, despite her lack of previous work in the area.

While it may seem self-evident that second-language students should seek to maximize their opportunities to interact in English with both native and non-native speakers, within the university and without, research into acculturation suggests that being supported by a community of co-nationals, particularly in the early stages, can help with transition issues (Al-Sharideh and Goe 1998; Myles and Cheng 2003; Sung 2000). It is certainly the case that international students desire contact with locals, and particularly with native speakers of English, and this is to be encouraged. Supervisors should however bear in mind that the local community of fellow country people may have a role to play in assisting the new student settle in and they may want to try to facilitate this contact, through, for example, linking the student to a national society on the campus. Supervisors should be aware of the role that informal social networks can play in facilitating student adjustment, particularly when there are a number of students from the same country who already participate in these networks. These can help with accommodation, child and spousal support, as well as providing informal mentoring. Humphrey and McCarthy (1999) found that students from countries with few students studying at their university tended to have the most unrealistic expectations as they were not able to benefit from advice from returning students or from existing informal networks on arrival in terms of accommodation and settling in. Bradley (2000: 428) reports that a student in the UK told her that 'students need the empathy and under-standing from their own country' as locals appeared initially, but ultimately superficially, friendly. It is also important that students understand that the new environment is in fact a multicultural one, where the norm is that stu-dents and supervisors from a range of cultural and linguistic backgrounds interact on a daily basis and that this presents a unique opportunity (Myles and Cheng 2003).

Sung contrasts two very different student experiences:

> We have an international lab. The majority is internationals, including my advisor. We have two Indian girls, 2–3 American guys, 2 Taiwanese guys, and other internationals. The atmosphere is relaxing. Some of my good friends are from the lab because we work every day together ... We have a lot of fun.
>
> (Taiwanese student in Chemistry, third year of doctoral programme; cited in Sung 2000: 182)

> Typically, I eat, sleep, spend time with my wife, and study. I don't social-ize with Americans ... I went out of class immediately after class is dismissed ... We attend Chinese church ... This is the primary social activity I have. I don't attend departmental activities. I don't have a sense of belonging because of my English and stutter ...
>
> (Taiwanese student in Industrial Health, third year of doctoral programme; cited in Sung 2000: 120)

Application

Consider the tips provided below. Allow yourself to reflect on their rel-evance to you and your students. Having read these tips, do you think you might change the way you interact with students from different cultural or language backgrounds to your own in the future? List some changes you would like to make.

Tips for increasing your cross-cultural sensitivity: recommendations for supervisors

- Orientate yourself to pick up information about other cultures. This can simply be a matter of keeping your eyes and ears open and does not nec-essarily involve a great outlay of time. It can involve reading books or attending social events run by or for students from diverse cultural back-grounds.
- Be aware of practices which may be subtly excluding second-language students from full participation in research culture and other networks.

- Be aware of cultural issues and of how they can lead to misunderstandings between supervisors and second-language students.
- Examine your implicit assumptions about second-language students; try to make them explicit and then question their validity.
- Initiate exploration with your second-language research students to clarify the meanings behind any verbal or non-verbal communication which makes you uncomfortable. Check your accent and speech patterns are being understood.
- Show an interest in the welfare of your second-language research students, but find out about appropriate support services so that you can refer to them should that become necessary. Be aware that some international students may be unfamiliar with counselling services and reluctant to make use of the university's formal support services.
- At the outset of each second-language student's research programme, devote specific attention to negotiating the respective roles of the supervisor and student and your mutual expectations (see Figure 2.2).

(based on Cryer and Okorocha 1999: 117)

'Together we built a bridge that I could cross': 'hands-on' supervision

Mei's choice of words to describe the outcome of her relationship with her second supervisor, as the joint construction of a bridge she felt able to cross, epitomizes the positive qualities of a successful supervisory relationship (Aspland 1999: 34). The study of supervisory practice referred to at the beginning of this chapter noted that 'hands-on' supervision was associated with a greater number of completions in minimum time (Sinclair 2005). The practices of 'hands-on' supervisors would seem particularly appropriate for assisting second-language students and are explicitly referred to as essential in a number of studies of second-language thesis and dissertation writers (e.g. Belcher 1994; Braine 2002; Swales 2004). Supervisors need not feel they are engaging in excessive 'handholding'; at the heart of supervision is a relationship that must be negotiated. The second-language student and the supervisor can both benefit from an explicit conversation about mutual expectations, roles and responsibilities. The key characteristics of hands-on supervision are described below.

For all students, the first year is seen as vital for the establishment of this relationship. For the supervisor of the second-language student, hands-on engagement is imperative. The production of text is also essential from the beginning as it allows for early identification of problem areas in comprehension and writing, and candidates will benefit from regular and timely feedback. Hands-on supervisors provide more input earlier in the candidature and less input later. They constantly encourage and assist candidates to:

- draft thesis text;
- publish and present their research in journals and at conferences;
- go through a number of iterations of thesis and publication drafts.

(Sinclair 2005)

Hands-on supervisors establish 'consistent and viable relationships' based on the 'achievement of early and lasting agreement between supervisor's and candidate's expectations of each other' (Sinclair 2005: vii). These include negotiating a firm timetable for completion, particularly in relation to:

- available support and project logistics;
- institutional quality checks such as reviews;
- project-specific milestones such as the production of thesis text;
- the presentation and publication of conference and journal papers.

In other words, the relationship moves from being one of informal comradeship to a more professionalized one in which mutual expectations are clearly articulated without necessarily losing the dimensions of trust which are also important. Linguistic and cultural issues referred to earlier suggest that the onus to initiate and follow through with such discussion lies clearly with the supervisor at the commencement of study. Adams and Cargill (2003) report on a supervisor who tries to avoid potential miscommunication by asking students to email her an outline of the main issues discussed and actions agreed on by both parties after their meetings. They also suggest that supervisors get to know their students personally so that they can be aware of daily life issues that may affect the students' research, while noting that this strategy is not viewed favourably by all supervisors.

Application: the role perception scale

The role perception scale is a simple instrument to help both student and supervisor begin an open discussion about their potentially differing understandings of the supervisory relationship. We suggest that student and supervisor complete it separately and then compare their respective perceptions.

Read each pair of statements listed in Figure 2.2. Each expresses a point of view that supervisors and students may take. You may not agree fully with either of the statements; in this case, estimate your position and mark it on the scale. For example, if you believe very strongly that supervisors should select the research topic, you would circle '1' on scale 1. If you think that the supervisor and the student should be equally involved, then circle '3' and if you think it is definitely the student's responsibility to select a topic, circle '5'.

Topic/area of study		
1. It is a supervisor's responsibility to select a promising topic.	1 2 3 4 5	It is a student's responsibility to select a promising topic.
2. In the end, it is up to the supervisor to decide which theoretical frame of reference is most appropriate.	1 2 3 4 5	A student has the right to choose a theoretical standpoint even if it conflicts with that of the supervisor.
3. A supervisor should direct a student in the development of an appropriate programme of research and study.	1 2 3 4 5	A student should be able to work out a schedule and research programme appropriate to their needs.
4. A supervisor should ensure that a student has access to all necessary facilities, materials and support.	1 2 3 4 5	Ultimately, the student must find the necessary facilities, materials and support to complete their research.
Contact/involvement		
5. Supervisor–student relationships are purely professional and personal relationships should not develop.	1 2 3 4 5	Close personal relationships are essential for successful supervision.
6. A supervisor should initiate meetings with a student.	1 2 3 4 5	A student should initiate meetings with their supervisor.
7. A supervisor should check constantly that a student is on track and working consistently.	1 2 3 4 5	Students should have the opportunity to find their own way without having to account for how they spend their time.
8. A supervisor should terminate the candidature if they think a student will not succeed.	1 2 3 4 5	A supervisor should support the student regardless of their opinion of the student's capability.
The thesis/dissertation		
9. A supervisor should ensure that the thesis/dissertation is finished within the allocated time.	1 2 3 4 5	As long as a student works steadily they should be able to take as long as they need to finish the work.
10. A supervisor has direct responsibility for the methodology and content of the thesis/dissertation.	1 2 3 4 5	A student has total responsibility for ensuring that the methodology and content of the thesis/dissertation are appropriate to the discipline.
11. A supervisor should assist in the actual writing of the thesis/ dissertation if the student has difficulties, and should ensure that the presentation is flawless.	1 2 3 4 5	A student must take full responsibility for presentation of the thesis/dissertation, including grammar and spelling.
12. A supervisor should insist on seeing drafts of every section of the thesis/dissertation in order to give students feedback on their work	1 2 3 4 5	It is up to a student to ask for feedback from their supervisors.

Figure 2.2 The role perception scale
Source: based on Moses 1992: 25

Miò Bryce (2003), who is from a Japanese background, has reflected on her experience as both a PhD candidate and an academic in Australia, and recommends that the supervisor adopt a hands-on approach from early on, particularly given that many Asian students have come from a very supportive, structured environment and need to be supported towards autonomy and independence. Her advice is summarized below.

Tips for hands-on supervision in the initial stages

1   The aims and expectations of candidature should be articulated and agreed upon by both parties early on. In the initial stages these include:

- substantial discussions between supervisor and student to build a trusting and respectful relationship;
- articulation of roles and responsibilities;
- agreement on a timetable and a realistic framework;
- orientation of the student to support, including language support and research training;
- discussion of the supervisor's availability and means of contact;
- agreement on methods of monitoring progress.

2   Hold individual or group meetings to check accuracy of students' comprehension of reading materials in their areas of interest and to develop critical/analytical discussion skills. This may help with the transition from descriptive to analytical writing.
3   Encourage students to make notes in dot form or a paragraph to ensure they clarify the outline of their thinking and sentence structure.
4   Oral discussion skills are very important and may require explicit development.
5   Consider referral to language advising/editing services early as language is developmental and cannot simply be addressed through preliminary language courses. Language proficiency tests are entry-level only and assess types of writing that are very different to that of a research thesis.

(adapted from Bryce 2003)

Once the relationship is established, an open-door policy helps maintain it, with the supervisor regularly initiating contact with the student. Another key element is the establishment of a relationship of 'personal trust' which enables the supervisor to intervene appropriately if the candidate is experiencing difficulties and to refer the student to appropriate resources. The hands-on supervisor recognizes that there is an unequal power relationship between student and supervisor but uses his or her power to mentor the student's professional development as the student establishes him- or herself as a peer (Sinclair 2005: vii).

Mentorship, which involves a type of apprenticeship learning, collabora-tion in research and writing, and the establishment of trusting relationships, has been identified as a key component of successful supervision in a number of studies of second-language research students (Belcher 1994; Braine 2002; Dong 1997; Hasrati 2005; Myles and Cheng 2003). In Belcher's (1994) study of three second-language PhD students in the US and their mentors, the most successful of the student–supervisor relationships was observed to be less hierarchical, while being trust-based and supportive. While the supervisor still retained her authority, the successful student grew and developed the ability to become an independent researcher, in some ways surpassing her supervisor's expectations.

Su Wu's (2002) analysis of her experience of two very different postgraduate environments in the UK underlines what she perceives as Taiwanese students' need for explicit, hands-on, supportive supervision. Su Wu came to study in the UK from the highly structured, competitive, teacher-directed Taiwanese education system in which the traditional teacher 'filled the pot' (the empty student). She began her MPhil studies at an 'ancient' (her words) university where teaching tended to be conceptualized as simply 'lighting the fire' in the student, and then she enrolled at a new polytechnic university for her PhD. She contrasts these two experiences, describing the shock she and her fellow Chinese students experienced at the 'ancient' university, which appeared to lack structure and support and did not articulate its expectations of students, all in the name of cultivating the 'independence' and the maturity of post-graduate students. The polytechnic, on the other hand, provided her with the explicit induction, support and structure she needed for her doctoral studies.

Another characteristic of hands-on supervision that may particularly support the second-language student and reduce potential isolation and lack of access to academic research networks is the encouragement of team-work environments that:

- foster collaboration between candidates via informal coursework, seminars and use of electronic media;
- draw in other academics and experts;
- link candidates into broader research community and/or industry networks;
- encourage joint preparation for conference and journal papers.

(Sinclair 2005: viii)

While these sorts of environments are common in the sciences they are much less so in the social sciences and arts and, as identified earlier in this chapter, social and emotional isolation is a common experience for many PhD students (Deem and Brehony 2000; Delamount et al. 1997) and may be more acutely experienced by international second-language students far from friends and family. Dong (1998) comments that many supervisors are not aware of their second-language students' sense of isolation. Delamount *et al.* recommend providing access to facilities such as a staff common room and some social events where students and faculty can meet and socialize, while being sensitive to the needs of those who may not drink alcohol or may have childcare responsibilities. Second-language students need assistance with understanding the ways they can 'maximize the benefits to be derived from supervision, research training, reading groups, seminars and participation in learned societies' and a clearer understanding of 'what doctoral study is about' (Deem and Brehony 2000: 163). Some international social sciences students interviewed by Deem and Brehony would have welcomed 'more collective ways of working':

> You see, we don't have a common room ... where we could sit and talk and ... which is normal. I mean, my other university ... I mean you always bump into people in the coffee room [...] and you always can have a little chat with somebody in the coffee room and they say 'how are you doing' and 'how are you getting on'.
>
> (International student, cited in Deem and Brehony 2000: 158)

Supervisors can help international students by providing stability, structure and continuity, and by acknowledging the investment that students have made in coming to study in a foreign county, as well as their strong desire for success combined with the social and family pressures that are often heavier than those of English students (Wu 2002).

The introduction of research training courses at British and Australian universities may help with both transition and social network issues and they may parallel, to a limited extent, the substantial coursework that North American doctoral students complete before proceeding to the dissertation. Our own courses in thesis writing that run over a semester provide not only skills development but also an opportunity for students to interact across disciplinary boundaries and build collegial friendships (Paltridge 2003; Starfield 2003). Deem and Brehony (2000) found that the international students they surveyed appreciated the research training courses and felt them to be more beneficial than did the local students, both in terms of social contact and for skills and theoretical framework development:

> it was a very good experience ... In my country I felt everything was so new, ontology, epistemology and all new and different concepts going round in my head so having another year of methods course made a lot of difference because you settle down. [...] nowadays I go a lot back to my notes, especially those from the sessions about philosophy of social research.
>
> (Deem and Brehony 2000: 157)

Cohort or group supervision, which is the common and frequently very successful way supervision occurs in the natural sciences, fosters collaboration and communication and could be considered across all disciplines, particularly as a means of integrating second-language students into specific research cultures (Sinclair 2005). In Chapter 3, we consider the role that writing groups and learning how to provide feedback on the writing of others may help develop thesis writing skills.

Conclusion

While many of the issues that confront second-language students in the transition to the role of postgraduate student are similar to those that the native speaker of English may be facing, the costs for the second-language speaker will tend to be higher, both financially and in terms of the challenges they may encounter, a number of which have been outlined in this chapter. There is much that the proactive supervisor can do to alleviate these costs and we have suggested a number of strategies that might usefully be adopted. The words of a second-language speaker who is successfully working as an academic in an Australian university sum up the ideal that we all strive for:

> Doctoral supervision is a profound and lengthy joint venture involving both the supervisor and student, to nurture the development of a competent, autonomous researcher and to explore, and make a contribution to, the global academic environment. It is a demanding yet rewarding once in a lifetime experience involving two individuals' interactive, complete personal and professional commitment.

> (Bryce 2003: 6)

Chapter 3

Thesis writing in English as a second language

Introduction

All students writing a research thesis face the new challenge of having to manage large amounts of text across a lengthy period of time; 80,000 words is the typical length of a doctoral thesis in Britain or Australia. Prior's (1998) in-depth study of graduate students writing within their disciplines clearly demonstrates that even successful students struggle with writing at an advanced level; it is both quantitatively and qualitatively a different task to their previous experiences of academic writing. This challenge is heightened for the second-language speaker as they may struggle simultaneously in several domains, all of which have been identified as influencing academic writing at an advanced level. This chapter discusses four clusters of issues which can directly impact on the second-language-speaker writing a thesis in English. We have grouped them under four headings and will examine each of these in turn. They are:

- psycho-affective issues;
- behavioural issues;
- rhetorical issues (how language and the conventions of thesis writing are used to persuade the reader of the validity of the writer's arguments);
- social issues.

While these four factors may impact on the native-English-speaking thesis writer, it is their intensity and co-occurrence in combination with limited linguistic resources in English which may make the second-language thesis writer's task and, therefore, the supervisor's task, more arduous. To what extent are these factors part of the supervisor's brief? They may not directly appear to be but, if unacknowledged, may be contributing to either a lack of progress or failure to complete.

Psycho-affective/emotional issues

Under this heading a cluster of related issues can be grouped which may directly affect a student's ability to write. These are a lack of confidence, what is called the 'impostor syndrome', and fear of failure and rejection, or its counter-part perfectionism. The unifying thread in all of these psycho-affective issues that may lead to 'writer's block' or the inability to write is the fear the writer has that they are not competent to write a research thesis; they are an impostor who will be 'found out' and unmasked. The impostor syndrome may affect the second-language speaker more acutely for the reasons outlined in Chapter 2, particularly if, in the student's thinking, intellectual ability and language proficiency are in some way equated. Similarly, anxiety about potential failure or rejection of the thesis can become paralysing for the international student for whom, as pointed out in the previous chapter, the stakes are that much higher. The other side of the anxiety coin is the desire to write the 'perfect' thesis, which can be just as paralysing, especially when submission draws nearer. Those second-language students who tend to perfectionism may struggle with writing in English and experience anxiety about error.

The supervisor should be alert for the potential of the above issues to affect progress on the thesis. We have found it useful to discuss the impostor syndrome with students as an issue – the relief that students experience is often palpable as they realize they are not unique in this regard. They need to know that they would not have been accepted into the programme were they considered incompetent. Our students are often relieved to hear that very few students actually 'fail' a PhD and to be reminded that 'it's a PhD, not a Nobel Prize' – a quote from one of the experienced examiners interviewed by Mullins and Kiley (2002) in their article with the same title which looked at how experienced examiners assess research theses.

Murray (2002) points out that fear of the supervisor's feedback or fear of the supervisor him- or herself can also have an effect on the student's ability to write. Often this fear is related less to something the supervisor may have done but more to the student's own image of the supervisor as a punishing and judging figure. Unfortunately, fear may lead to avoidance behaviour by the student, thus depriving him or her of a valuable source of improvement. Riazi (1997) found that the Iranian doctoral students he interviewed reported that their supervisor's feedback was extremely helpful in their English language development. His study illustrates that the supervisor's comments were regarded as a significant resource for improving not only the content and ideas but also language use and the rhetorical organization of their writing.

Our advice is to schedule regular meetings, to give clear, comprehensible, constructive and above all actionable feedback (i.e. that the student can act on) appropriate to the writing stage the student is at. Discuss written feedback with your student to ensure they understand your comments. Explain the meanings of specific terms you use when you provide feedback so that you can develop a common language with your student in this regard. Encourage a climate in which they feel able to ask what your feedback means if they are not sure. Allow challenge. Allow them to tape-record your sessions in the initial stages while they become accustomed to your accent, intonation and general speech patterns. Consider Murray's suggestion that students attach to their draft a cover sheet that outlines:

- the purpose of what they have written;
- the kind of feedback they are seeking on this specific piece of writing;
- how they have responded to your previous feedback.

(Murray 2002: 202)

Remember the *Traditional Feedback Sandwich* when giving feedback:

- first the good news (what and why in detail);
- then the bad news (suggestions on how to overcome it);
- finally a note of encouragement.

A final suggestion for those students who are able to discuss their topic and put forward their arguments quite coherently orally but who experience great difficulty with writing is to ask them to talk into a tape recorder and then have them edit the typed transcript. We have found this approach has helped several of our students to 'unblock'.

The three factors discussed below are different in that they provide ways of responding to the psycho-affective issues raised here.

Behavioural issues

Many students struggle with writing as they labour under the romantic belief that writing is a creative and spontaneous act of inspiration: that they can write only when the 'muse' descends. However, as Zerubavel (1999) persuasively argues in his highly recommended study of successful writers, writing needs to become a habit. It is paradoxically through writing regularly, ideally on a daily basis, that the 'muse' – inspiration – comes, hence the title of his book, *The Clockwork Muse*. It is most important that the second-language writer under-stands the need to 'write early and write often'. Text production leads to more text production. One of the greatest obstacles to students' writing is the little phrase 'writing up' – which leads to students putting off writing until such time as the research is perceived to be 'done'. Your students need to see writing as an integral part of the research process and to be encouraged to write from early on in this process, whether it be initially through notes and reflections, through logs and diaries or through early drafts of a literature review. For the second-language speaker, this is vital as the skills of writing are acquired devel-opmentally over time and language continues to develop incrementally.

Introducing students to the idea of writing as a process can be extremely helpful. We have found Figures 3.1 and 3.2 (on pp.46 and 47) very enlight-ening to our students as they realize the amount and extent of revision that experienced and successful writers undertake. Figure 3.1 illustrates how early studies of the processes writers go through as they write conceptualized writing as a process involving prewriting or planning, drafting, getting feedback, revising and then editing before 'submitting'.

More recently, research has demonstrated the even greater complexity of the processes we engage in when writing (see Figure 3.2), highlighting the non-linear nature of writing and the multiple iterations involved. The usefulness of this research for second-language thesis writers is that it helps break a highly complex set of processes into a series of simpler stages or sub-tasks which enable them to 'get started' and have a sense of accomplishment as these smaller tasks are completed. They also become aware of the key role of feedback and the essential role of revising and that there will be times at which they may need to redraft (go back closer to the beginning). Extensive drafting and feedback should also effectively reduce potential plagiarism as the writer will be receiving feedback on a continuous basis.

Academic writing at an advanced level is therefore more than 'just getting ideas down on paper' and being sure that they are in 'good English' (Atkinson and Curtis 1998: 17). What student writers need to grasp is that there is a reciprocal relationship between thinking and writing (see Figure 3.3). Writing is an essential means of clarifying our thoughts which is why delaying writing can become an obstacle to the development of understanding and why, conversely, regular writing facilitates the development of understanding of a topic.

Biggs *et al.* (1999) point out that second-language writers may be spending proportionately too much of their time on the mechanics of writing – on sentence, grammar and word-level features – rather than on generating meaning at a higher level and then organizing it into sentences and finding the

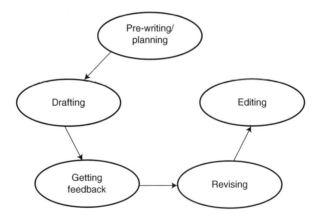

Figure 3.1 A simplified model of the writing process

Source: Atkinson and Curtis 1998

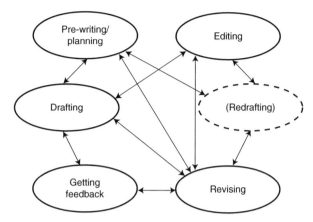

Figure 3.2 A more realistic model of the writing process
Source: Atkinson and Curtis 1998

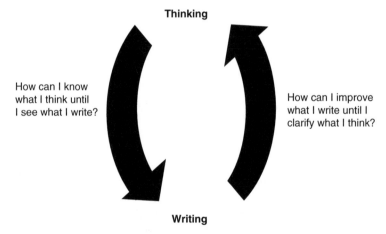

Figure 3.3 The reciprocal relationship of writing and thinking
Source: Huff 1999: 7

appropriate words. The overarching themes of the writing may then be lost and unsupported and sections of text become irrelevant even though well written at a sentence level. They suggest encouraging students to generate text and revise and edit it later, which may reduce blocking.

Murray (2002) recommends a very useful strategy for encouraging students to generate text, particularly in the early stages of the PhD. She suggests using the following set of prompts to help student write about the context of their topic. They can be used repeatedly as the student's focus develops or alters:

What can I write about? The context/background to my research

> My research question is .... (50 words)
> Researchers who have looked at this subject are .... (50 words)
> They argue that .... (25 words)
> Researcher A argues that .... (25 words)
> Researcher B argues that .... (25 words)
> Debate centres on the issue of .... (25 words)
> There is still work to be done on .... (25 words)
> My research is closest to that of Researcher A in that .... (50 words)
> My contribution will be .... (50 words)
>
> (Murray 2002: 98)

Rhetorical issues

For many, writing a thesis will be the first time they have had to manage and structure such a large amount of text. Dong argues that writing a thesis or a dissertation is a

> most formidable task for many graduate students. [...] not only because of the daunting size of the document but also because of the high standard to which the thesis/dissertation is held. The writing challenge is not only demonstrating knowledge related to the research but also using that knowledge to 'argue logically and coherently the meaning of the research results'.
>
> (Dong 1998: 369)

Biggs *et al.* (1999) and Torrance and Thomas (1994) found that native and non-native thesis writers benefited from explicit instruction on how to structure a thesis and its constituent parts. These findings are supported by extensive research into academic writing that emphasizes the importance of explicit teaching of the structure of specific written genres, particularly to second-language students. Much supervisor knowledge of writing is tacit and, although supervisors recognize 'good writing', they often find difficulty in explaining to their students how to get there. As Tardy (2005: 326) points out, the advanced academic literacy needed by research students requires not only linguistic ability but 'rhetorical insight' into their 'disciplinary community's ways of building and disseminating information'. One of the fundamental aims of this book is to assist supervisors to better advise their students in understanding the generic and rhetorical structuring of the thesis, and this is the focus of subsequent chapters.

Flowerdew (1999) noted that Hong Kong Chinese scholars attempting to publish in English experienced difficulty in a number of areas including length of time to compose in English; facility with English expression; extent and richness of vocabulary; and making claims for their research that had the requisite degree of force and the influence of their mother tongue. They felt that their language skills limited them to a simple style of writing; they perceived writing qualitative research to be more challenging than quantitative research and found writing the Introductions and Discussion sections of research articles to be particularly difficult. While Flowerdew interviewed academics who had completed a doctorate and who were writing for publication, the issues he examines are equally pertinent for non-native speakers of English who are writing a doctoral or master's thesis.

As Angelova and Riazantseva (1999) note, international postgraduate students' previous experience of writing extended texts may be limited, as well as their experience of selecting a topic where previously all topics have been assigned. Students in the social sciences and humanities may struggle with topic choices, while for students in the sciences and engineering it is more common for the supervisor to have an influence on the choice of topic.

Dunleavy (2003) underlines the importance for the thesis writer of managing reader expectations and always writing with the reader in mind. Students from a range of linguistic backgrounds may experience difficulty with the degree of explicit guidance to the reader that characterizes academic English prose. English (and certain other languages such as Norwegian) have been described as 'writer-responsible' in that 'English speakers, by and large, charge the writer, or speaker, with the responsibility to make clear and well-organized statements' (Hinds 1987: 143). In contrast, writers of languages which tend to be more 'reader-responsible', such as French or Polish or some Asian languages, may perceive the direction, signalling and signposting to the reader required in a lengthy thesis insulting to the intelligence of their reader as they imagine him or her. Our second-language students find the notion of writer responsibility very helpful in the structuring of their writing (see also Chapter 1).

A key way in which writers acknowledge their responsibility is through their use of metadiscourse (also referred to as metatext) which can be described as the writer's overt acknowledgement of the reader (Dahl 2004). Metadiscourse primarily plays the role of organizing the text for the reader and is used by the writer to interact with the reader about the content of the text. Second-language students need to be exposed to this feature of language, specifically the ways in which the lengthy text of the thesis needs previews, reviews and overviews to assist the reader in making sense of the structure and arguments. The following extract illustrates the way in which the writer of a PhD thesis in linguistics concludes her chapter with a brief summary and then previews the following chapter, providing useful signposting for the reader.

7.3 Conclusion

This chapter has been concerned with methodologies for discovering patterns of preference for interpersonal values, arguing strongly for the usefulness of the Appraisal framework to describe the interpersonal meanings of a register such as school history. In Chapter 8, I will show how such a method of analysis can make important contributions to our understandings of the interpretative nature of history generally and the writing of school students specifically.

(from Coffin 2000: 289)

The concept of metadiscourse is discussed at greater length in subsequent chapters and illustrated in many of the annotated examples in later chapters of this book.

Johnston's findings from her study of 51 examiners' reports of doctoral theses provide further evidence of the expectations the reader/examiner of the thesis has and the importance of signposting in the thesis. Some of her key findings are summarized below:

- Examiners approach reading a thesis with an air of expectation and even enthusiasm, but this disappears if the thesis is not *reader-friendly*.
- General impression and overall presentation of the thesis seems particularly important to the examiners.
- The reader needs to be assisted through the use of summaries, logical sequencing, signposts and the removal of excessive repetition.
- *All* readers require assistance to understand the work; they feel distracted and irritated by poorly presented work; they appreciate well-written, interesting and logically presented arguments.

(Johnston 1997: 340)

Relatedly, the second-language students studied by Shaw (1991) struggled with the notion of audience: for whom were they writing their thesis? What was the image of the reader they had in mind as they wrote? Whereas undergraduate students clearly know they are writing to be assessed and therefore need to display their knowledge of the topic, regardless of the fact that the marker will know all about the topic, the thesis writer has a more complex relationship to his or her audience, in effect caught between 'knowledge-display and information-transmission' (Shaw 1991: 193). In fact, the real and most immediate readers (or audience) of the thesis will be the supervisor and the external examiners who will already know much about the topic. Thesis writers then must, to some extent, display their knowledge of the field, though in a more sophisticated and elaborated way than an undergraduate. They are not simply communicating as one expert to another or communicating with a non-specialist with some background knowledge but are writing to persuade an expert that they are worthy of joining a community of scholars. Shaw found that supervisor confusion in this regard might be adding to student lack of certainty. This confusion impacts on the thesis writer's sense of identity as they straddle the border between being a student and being a peer. If they are simultaneously writing journal articles for publication, they will need to adopt a more 'expert' sounding voice, whereas in the thesis they may 'sound' more like a student, albeit a 'sophisticated' one. How to sound both authoritative and deferent is a challenge, more especially in a language that is not your first language. It is very important that the supervisor and the student discuss the notion of audience or readership in terms of both writer responsibility and the specific rhetorical (persuasive) aims of a thesis.

In her study of a second-language master's student's development as a successful thesis writer, Tardy (2005) shows how Paul (the student) revised his text as he became more aware of the need to explicitly persuade his reader of the logic of his argument. She quotes him as saying:

> one thing I learned from this is when I wrote something quite long, I *must* make it *clear* that what I try to express is interesting to readers. I cannot just put lots of experimental results in my writing without explaining what's the importance of this result and why we should care about this experiment.
>
> (Tardy 2005: 332)

Further compounding the issue of how authoritative to sound is finding the appropriate 'voice' in English. As Hirvela and Belcher (2001) point out, many of the second-language writers who enrol in postgraduate study are already successful writers in their first language and have established a strong sense of self as a writer in this language or, in fact, in several languages. However, limited language resources can mean that writing a thesis in English and 'sounding like' the sort of person they wish to sound like becomes extremely threatening and frustrating. Established professionals or academics in their home country can experience 'extreme difficulty [...] making the transition from holding a position of professional respect in the native country to the anonymous and relatively powerless life of a graduate student in the new country' (Hirvela and Belcher 2001: 99). Finding an appropriate academic 'voice' can also prove difficult for students from politically repressive regimes who may have difficulty expressing critical perspectives or their own opinion – a standard expectation of western anglophone universities (Angelova and Riazantseva 1999).

Finding an academic voice in English may be more challenging than the supervisor can imagine. Shen, who moved from China to study in North America, insightfully captures the extent of the conflict a student may experience as they struggle to find an academic English 'voice' and the implications for their sense of self. He eventually arrived at an innovative resolution of his sense of having to become a different person when writing in English:

First I made a list of (simplified) features about writing associated with my old identity (the Chinese Self), [...] and then beside the first list I added a column of features about writing associated with my new identity (the English Self). After that I pictured myself getting out of my old identity, the timid, humble, modest Chinese 'I' and creeping into my new identity (often in the form of a new skin or a mask), the confident, assertive, and aggressive English 'I'.

(Shen 1989: 462)

It is important that supervisors empathize with potential issues of self and identity that students may be experiencing, which can impact on their writing.

Furthermore, thesis writers need to understand that they will be evaluated by their readers (examiners) in their own terms – in terms of the claims they make in their argument. Mullins and Kiley (2002: 385) found that experienced examiners are careful to check for links between the Introduction, in which students state their intentions, and the Conclusion 'where the intentions should have been realised'. Moderating their claims becomes very important as they should neither 'boost' their claims too strongly, or overgeneralize, nor should they fail to make them with the appropriate force to convince the reader of the value of the claim being made. This is where the linguistic resources known as 'hedges' become extremely important to the second-language thesis writer as they learn how to adjust the strength of their claims in relation to their audience and communicative purpose. Hedging is discussed in more detail in Chapters 9 and 10.

In Shaw's (1991: 195–196) study, the students reported that using semitechnical vocabulary and finding the right word for the context were their areas of greatest difficulty. However, he found that many of the students had developed a strategy of extensive reading in their subject area followed by note-making of useful terms that they could use in their own writing. Phrases such as 'the foregoing indicates'; 'highlighted the fact that'; and 'such tests are still useful but it is now recognised that' would be noted down and reused. One of the Russian students interviewed by Angelova and Riazantseva (1999) made lists of words and phrases that she could use to introduce topics, build arguments, agree or disagree with a position, and close a discussion. This strategy helped her when she felt unable to write. Encouraging second-language students to read not only for content but also to pay attention to the ways expert writers of books and articles structure their texts in the way Shaw's students did can help them expand their linguistic resources. Similarly, encouraging them to use features of their word-processing program such as an online thesaurus can help build vocabulary.

Applications

1   Discuss the notion of 'writer-responsible' text with your student. Ask them to reflect on their first language in terms of how writer-responsible it might be and how this might impact on their academic writing.

2   Ask your student to examine three recent theses in your field. Ask them to consider the following:

- Are they reader-friendly? If so, what features make them so?
- How do the writers refer to themselves? Which style does your student prefer and why?
- How do they want to 'sound' when they write?

Social issues

The solitary nature of writing a thesis and its potential for isolation are well known. As we have shown in Chapter 2, second-language students may be particularly vulnerable in this regard, particularly if their isolation affects their ability to receive and benefit from feedback during the process of writing. Shaw's (1991: 193) findings as noted in the previous section show that the second-language thesis writers he interviewed were not making use of 'feedback from colleagues as a resource in the writing process', either for revising or for editing. What role does the supervisor have in providing a supportive environment? Research indicates that peer support groups and group feedback may indeed help not only with combating potential isolation but also to assist with writing development. In a study of 45 doctoral students, Caffarella and Barnett (2000) found that preparing critiques for their peers and receiving critiques from professors and peers were the most significant elements in helping them to understand the processes of scholarly writing and in improving their academic writing. They conclude that although the processes of learning to give and receive feedback may be stressful, the frustrations are outweighed by the benefits derived from participating in a sustained writing development programme which incorporates instruction on how to provide explicit feedback in conjunction with receiving feedback from faculty members and fellow students.

Building a culture in your department or school in which PhD students meet regularly and are encouraged to read and comment on short extracts from one another's work could be a valuable contribution to the writing development of your students. Alternatively, as many universities now offer thesis-writing courses via a centrally-based learning centre or writing centre, recommend to your students that they attend such a course. Students will then have the opportunity to engage with students from differing disciplines or schools and will be able to talk to one another about their research and writing. The social dimension provided by this type of instruction can be almost as important as the writing instruction. For example, public discussion of writing and anxiety can relieve an individual's sense of isolation and inadequacy.

Conclusion

This chapter has examined four issues which can affect the ability of the second-language writer to successfully complete a thesis. Not all may appear immediately relevant to writing but there is now a significant body of research, some of it reported on in this chapter, that indicates that psycho-affective, behavioural and social issues as well as issues of the self and identity in a new language and culture can substantially influence a student's capacity to engage in and sustain writing over a lengthy period. Moreover, expectations about the relationship between writers and readers may vary across languages and cultures and may need to be explicitly discussed. It is important that the supervisor of the second-language student be aware of the potential for these issues to impact on the production of the thesis.

Chapter 4

Writing a research proposal

Introduction

Research proposals are an example of what Swales (1996) calls 'occluded' genres; that is, genres which are difficult for students to have to access to, but play an important part in the students' lives. In his book *Successful Dissertations and Theses*, Madsen (1992: 51) writes that 'the research proposal is often the key element to the successful thesis and, as such, the most important step in the whole process'. Meloy (1994: 31) presents a similar view, saying that 'proposal writing does not appear to be something that comes naturally' and that we learn not only by example but also by the reactions and suggestions of our supervisors and our thesis committee members. The process of writing a research proposal will, therefore, be examined in some detail in this chapter. Topics covered will include choosing and focusing a research topic, developing a research proposal, the structure and purpose of research proposals, details to include in a research proposal, differences between a master's and a doctoral thesis, and different expectations across different areas of study.

Differences between master's and doctoral theses

An important point for students to consider before they write their research proposal is the degree they are writing it for, and what that degree requires of them.

A number of writers have discussed differences in expectations between master's and doctoral theses, and their characterizing features (e.g. Madsen 1992; Elphinstone and Schweitzer 1998; Tinkler and Jackson 2000). It is important for students to understand these differences at the outset of their research project, as this will impact on the focus and scale of the project they plan to undertake, and, in turn, the research proposal they write.

As Madsen (1992) points out, generally a doctoral thesis has greater breadth, depth and intention than a master's thesis. Below is a summary of the distinction he makes between a master's dissertation and a doctoral thesis.

A master's dissertation demonstrates:

- an original investigation or the testing of ideas;
- competence in independent work or experimentation;
- an understanding of appropriate techniques as well as their limitations;
- an expert knowledge of the published literature on the topic under investigation;
- evidence of the ability to make critical use of published work and source materials;
- an appreciation of the relationship between the research topic and the wider field of knowledge;
- the ability to present the work at an appropriate level of literary quality.

A doctoral thesis demonstrates:

- all of the above, plus:
- a distinct contribution to knowledge, as shown by the topic under investigation, the methodology employed, the discovery of new facts, or interpretation of the findings.

In scope, the doctoral thesis differs from a master's research degree by its deeper, more comprehensive treatment of the subject under investigation (Elphinstone and Schweitzer 1998). A doctoral thesis is also required to demonstrate authority in the area of research. That is, the student is expected to have an expert and up-to-date knowledge of the area of study and research that is relevant to their particular topic. The thesis also needs to be written in succinct, clear, error-free English.

At the doctoral level, examiners are often asked whether the thesis contains material that is in some way worthy of publication. The issue of a 'distinct contribution to knowledge' is an important consideration at the doctoral level. In short, has the writer carried out a piece of work that demonstrates that a research apprenticeship is complete and that the student 'should be admitted to the community of scholars in the discipline?'

A study carried out by Tinkler and Jackson (2000) in Great Britain found that while there was a large amount of agreement among the criteria used by universities for defining doctoral theses, the actual examination of the thesis was often conceptualized, and carried out, in rather different ways. It is therefore important for students to be aware of the criteria their university will use for assessing their thesis.

Applications

1   Discuss Madsen's (1992) distinction between a master's dissertation and a doctoral thesis with your student as they are writing their research proposal. Tell them to return to these criteria once they have written their proposal and to ask themselves to what extent their proposal is for a piece of work that will meet these criteria.

2   Ask your student to look for their university's guidelines for the examination of theses and dissertations and the criteria that will be used for assessing them. Tell them to consider these criteria while writing their research proposal and to ask themselves in what way their project fits with the university's criteria.

A checklist for developing a research proposal

Nunan (1992) and Bell (1999) provide good advice for students writing a research proposal. The following checklist summarizes their work. This is a helpful list to work through with students as they are deciding on, and refining, their research topic.

(i)   Draw up a shortlist of topics. Students can do this, for example, by speaking to other students, asking colleagues, asking potential supervisors, or looking up related research in the library.
(ii) Select a topic for investigation.
(iii) Then, formulate a general question. That is, turn the topic into a research question.
(iv) Next, focus the question. That is, be as specific as possible about what the study will investigate. This is often difficult to do, so students should spend as much time as necessary to get their question right.

The question needs to be:

*   worth asking; that is, it needs to be *significant*;
*   capable of being answered; that is, it needs to be *feasible*.

There are many questions that are worth asking but which cannot, in any practical sense, be answered. It is important to strike a balance between the value of the question and the student's ability to develop a research proposal they are capable of carrying out; that is, a project that the student has the background and training required to carry out.

(v)   Decide on the aims and objectives of the study or formulate a hypothesis.
(vi) Think about the data that need to be collected to answer the question.

(vii) Draw up an initial research plan.
(viii) Now, read enough to be able to decide whether the project is on the right lines. Look especially at previous research in the area. Good places to look are journal articles, research reports and other theses and dissertations written in the area.
(ix) Next write up a detailed proposal, including definitions of key terms that are used in your proposal. That is, define the characteristics of the terms you used in the proposal in a way that would enable an outsider to identify them if they came across them.

Often a student starts off with a fairly brief proposal that is further refined over a period of time (Elphinstone and Schweitzer 1998). This depends on the requirements of the particular university and academic department and the particular requirements they set for students applying for admission to a degree and the writing of a research proposal within that degree. It is important for students to check these requirements and write a proposal that meets the requirements of the particular setting in which they are writing their proposal.

Refining a research question

Stevens and Asmar (1999) point out that often new researchers start off with a project that is overly large and ambitious. They suggest that 'wiser heads' know that a good thesis project is 'narrow and deep'. In their words, 'even the simplest idea can mushroom into an uncontrollably large project' (Stevens and Asmar 1999: 15). They highlight how important it is for students to listen to their supervisor and be guided by their advice in the early stages of their research.

Applications

• Ask your student to draw up a shortlist of possible research topics, writing a sentence or two about each one. Discuss this list with the student, suggesting issues that might arise with each of them, such as practicality, originality, focus and scale of the project, etc.
• Once your student has selected a topic from their list, ask them to carry out steps (iii) to (iv) in the checklist above and bring back what they have done for further discussion.
• Once this discussion has taken place, ask your student to read further on their topic (step (viii)). Give your student the following checklist (based on Stevens and Asmar 1999) to help with this:

Ways to refine a research question

- Read broadly and widely to find a subject about which you are passionate. Immerse yourself in the literature, use your library, read abstracts of other recent theses and dissertations, check theses on the web. For example:

  - http://www.ndltd.org/
  - http://wwwlib.umi.com/dissertations/

- Narrow your focus to a single question: be disciplined and not over-ambitious.
- Be prepared to change or modify your question if necessary.
- Be able to answer the question 'Why am I doing this project?' (and not a different one).
- Read up-to-date materials – ensure that your idea is achievable and no one else has done or is doing it.
- Consult other students who are further down the track, especially those who have the same supervisor as you.
- Discuss your ideas with your supervisor and lots of other people.
- Attend specialized conferences in your area – take note of the focus of research and learn from the experts in your field.
- Work through the implications of your research question: consider existing materials and ideas on which it is based, check the logic, spell out methods to be used.
- Condense your research question into two sentences, write them down, above your work area. Change the question if needed.
- Ask yourself: What will we know at the end that we did not already know?

Details to include in a research proposal

Below is a list of points that are often included in research proposals.

1   A clearly focused statement of the overall purpose of the proposed research.
2   A clearly focused research question/hypothesis that is:
    - worth asking;
    - capable of being answered.
3   Precise definitions of the key terms in the research question/s or hypothesis that will allow them to be clearly observed, measured and identified throughout the study.

4 An awareness of key research that has already been carried out in the particular area including:

- what conclusions were reached in this previous research, by whom and when;
- whether these conclusions are in agreement or conflict with each other;
- the main issues or controversies that surround the problem;
- significant gaps in previous research in this particular area;
- an indication of how this previous research is relevant to the proposed study.

5 An appropriate choice of research approach for the particular question or problem including a well-defined list of procedures to be followed in carrying out the research. This should include the method of data collection and analysis. The proposal should also include, if appropriate:

- a broad description of any particular theoretical framework to be used in the analysis and the reason/s for its use in the study;
- a brief statement describing how the sample population will be selected for the study and the reason for the approach to selection;
- a pilot study in which the research instruments will be trialled and evaluated and an analysis carried out of the trial data.

6 A section which highlights any anticipated problems and limitations in the proposed study including threats to reliability and validity and how these will be countered.

7 A statement which illustrates why the study is significant; that is, why the research question or hypothesis is worth asking.

8 Consideration of ethical issues involved in carrying out the research such as whether informed consent needs to be obtained, and if so, how this will be done.

9 A proposed timetable for the research. This is extremely important as it gives an indication as to how realistic the proposal actually is.

10 A proposed budget for the research (if appropriate). This is also important as it gives an indication of how realistic the proposal may be in terms of financial requirements and whether the research might need to be adapted in the light of these.

11 A list of references which relate to the proposal.

12 Appendices (if appropriate) which contain any material that will be used or adapted for the study, including any permission that might need to be obtained to use it.

There is a sample research proposal at the end of this book that students may wish to look at as a guide for what they might write.

Table 4.1 Purpose of each section of a research proposal

Section	Purpose
Title	To summarize, in a few words, what the research will be about
Summary	To provide an overview of the study which you will expand on in more detail in the text that follows.
Overall purpose	To present a clear and concise statement of the overall purpose of the research.
Relevant background literature	To demonstrate the relationship between the proposed study and what has already been done in the particular area; that is, to indicate the 'gap' that the study will fill.
Research question/s	To provide an explicit statement of what the study will investigate.
Definitions of terms	To provide the meaning of the key terms that have been used in the research question/s.
Research methodology	To give an illustration of the steps the project will go through in order to carry out the research.
Anticipated problems and limitations	To show awareness of the limitations of the study, what problems may be met in carrying it out, and how they will be dealt with.
Significance of the research	To say why the study is worth carrying out.
Resources required/budget	To say what resources the research will require – and what other costs may be anticipated in carrying out the study.
Ethics	To provide a statement as to how participants will be advised of the overall nature of the study, and how informed consent will be obtained from them.
Proposed table of contents	To give an overview of the scale and anticipated organization of the thesis or dissertation.
Timetable	To give a working plan for carrying out, and completing, the study.
References	To provide detailed references and bibliographic support for the proposal.
Appendix	To provide examples of materials that might be used, or adapted, in the study.

Application

Discuss the purpose of each section of a research proposal with your student. Table 4.1 may be helpful for this discussion.

Application

Ask your student to write a detailed research proposal using the following set of headings.

- Proposed title of the study
- Summary of the proposed study
- Purpose of the proposed study
- Relevant background literature
- Research question/s or hypotheses
- Definitions of terms
- Research methodology
- Significance of the research
- Ethical considerations
- Timetable for the research
- Anticipated problems and limitations
- Resources required for the research
- Bibliography
- Appendix

Application

When your student has written the first draft of their proposal, ask them
to look at the list of points presented earlier in this section (pp. 59–60)
and consider to what extent they have addressed each of them.

Criteria for assessing research proposals

In an article titled 'English for academic possibilities: the research proposal as
a contested site', Cadman (2002) surveyed and interviewed supervisors to ask
them to prioritize the particular features they expected to see in a research
proposal. She found supervisors gave most value to:

- the logic of the student's argument;
- a well-focused research question, set of research objectives, or hypothesis;
- the width and depth of the student's reading;
- the feasibility of the student's project;
- a critical approach to the literature;
- justification of the project through the literature;
- understanding of current issues on the student's topic;
- matching of methodology and methods to the research questions.

Application

Ask your student to consider their research proposal in relation to Cadman's set of criteria. Which part/s of the proposal could be improved? How?

Differences between disciplines in choosing a research topic

Many students do not realize that there are differences between the sciences, humanities and social sciences in terms of the kinds of research topics they can choose, the amount of freedom they will have in choosing their topic, the amount of guidance they will be given in writing their research proposal, and when they will be required to present their research proposal. For example, in the sciences, students often have a restricted range of topics to choose from for their proposal, especially if the topic is linked to a funded research project. In the humanities, students are usually required to initiate their own topics, taking into account supervisors' interests and the availability of data. In the social sciences and in professional fields of study, topics and research questions are often derived from the student's own professional practice. In the sciences, the students' research questions are often decided early on whereas in the social sciences the identification of specific research questions may take some time as students gain more disciplinary and methodological knowledge before they finally formulate their questions (Parry and Hayden 1996).

Swales (2004) points to other differences in expectations for research proposals, particularly across academic departments. For example, some departments may require a 100-page research proposal that includes data collection and analysis while others may ask for a review of the literature that points to a doable and worthwhile project. Other departments may ask for a proposal that follows the requirements of a particular external funding body. One thing that does not seem to make a difference, however, is the country in which the thesis is being written. Swales says that theses and dissertations seem to be little influenced by different national traditions and do not seem to have any typically distinct national characteristics, as opposed to the oral examination, or dissertation defence, which can vary markedly from one country to another (Johns and Swales 2002; Morley *et al.* 2002).

Applications

- Ask your student to consider: What amount of freedom are they allowed in choosing their topic in their area of study? How much guidance will they receive in choosing and refining their topic? When are they required to decide on their research topic? How extensive is their research proposal expected to be?
- Ask your student to choose one of the following chapters or articles, read it and write a summary of the key points discussed in it. Ask the student also to write about how these points relate to their own research project. Ask the student to bring back their piece of writing to discuss with you.
  - Mauch and Birch 1998: Chapter 4. This chapter discusses the preparation of a research proposal, including choosing a topic and assessing topic feasibility and practicability.
  - Madsen 1992: Chapter 4. This chapter discusses the statement of research problems, writing a literature review, developing research procedures, trial tables of contents, bibliographies and ethical considerations in carrying out research. The resources section of the book includes examples of a number of students' research proposals.
  - Davis and Parker 1997: Chapter 6. This chapter includes discussion on the choice of a research topic, the form of a research proposal, narrowing the scope and clarifying the purpose of a research proposal, and checking the feasibility of research procedures.
  - Meloy 1994: Chapter 3. This chapter discusses students' experiences in writing a proposal for a qualitative study. It also provides a list of guiding questions for developing a qualitative research proposal.
  - Bell 1999: Chapter 2. This chapter discusses planning a research project, selecting a topic, focusing the study and presenting a project outline.
  - Elphinstone and Schweitzer 1998: Chapter 1. This chapter ('Getting Started') is especially relevant to writing a research proposal. Section headings in this chapter include 'What is a thesis?', 'Distinction between a Master's and a Doctoral degree', 'Choosing a thesis topic', 'Defining your thesis topic', 'Methodology and research design', 'The research proposal', 'Criteria for assessing a research proposal' and 'Checklist of questions to be asked about a research proposal'.

- Locke *et al.* 2000. This book contains sample research proposals for experimental studies, quasi-experimental studies and qualitative studies.
- Paltridge 1997. This article describes a workshop aimed at helping second-language students write research proposals.

Conclusion

This chapter has discussed the writing of research proposals, an important stage in the thesis and dissertation writing process. The proposal students write becomes both a work plan for their further work and the basis of the text that will eventually become their thesis or dissertation. Different institutions place different levels of importance on the research proposal. While it may take a lot of time to write the proposal, it is worth spending as much time as is needed to get it right.

The proposal in the Appendix is an example of a proposal that a student wrote at the beginning of her candidature. As she continued with her research, her understanding of background theory became further developed, as did issues of methodology and analysis. The final title of her thesis also changed (to 'Style choice and sentence final particles in Japanese: directing interactions and constructing identity') as her project became more refined and more fully developed. This is very common and is something students should be made aware of. The proposal is the students' starting point in what may be end up being a somewhat different project from where it started. As Manalo and Trafford (2004: 76) observe, there are likely to be many deviations from what the students initially propose, as they 'make new discoveries and encounter unforeseen challenges over the course of the thesis-writing process'. The proposal is, however, a very important stage, 'along the dissertation road'.

Chapter 5

The overall shape of theses and dissertations

Introduction

Many second-language students are unaware of the recent evolution of thesis and dissertation types and the options this provides for them. There is, for example, an increasing number of qualitative and 'non-traditional' theses and dissertations being written. These present particular challenges in terms of how they should be written, as do theses and dissertations by publication. This chapter provides supervisors with examples of thesis and dissertation types, advice on guiding students with the overall structure of the thesis or dissertation, and the drafting of chapter outlines. It also introduces the concept of *metatext*, or 'text about the text', a key organizational tool for managing extended texts and for helping the reader follow the organization of the text.

A review of thesis and dissertation types

Nearly all of the literature on thesis and dissertation writing consists of handbooks and guides with, apart from a few notable exceptions, very little analysis having been carried out of actual texts. Atkinson (1997) suggests a number of reasons why this might be the case. The first of these is the accessibility of the texts; that is, theses and dissertations are often difficult to obtain in university libraries, and even more difficult to obtain from outside a university. It is only recently that they have come to be available electronically via online databases (see Chapter 12). Another difficulty is the sheer size of theses and dissertations as texts for analysis. This often limits what researchers can observe as well as the number of texts they are able to analyse. Further, there is often considerable variation in expectations across disciplines and fields of study (and indeed supervisors) in terms of what a thesis or dissertation should look like (Dudley-Evans 1993, 1999; Thompson 1999).

A further problem is that theses and dissertations in some areas of study are changing. For example, a thesis or dissertation written in certain areas of study may now be very different from one that might have been written ten or more years ago, particularly with the influence of what Hodge (1998: 113) terms the 'postmodern turn' in the 'new humanities' and social sciences. Thus, in some areas of study, theses and dissertations may be theorized, researched and written up in quite different ways from how they might have been in the past.

Although theses and dissertations are similar in some ways to other pieces of research writing, such as research articles, they are also in many ways quite different. Apart from the scale of the piece of writing, they also vary in terms of their purpose, readership, the kind of skills and knowledge they are required to demonstrate and 'display', and the kinds of requirements they need to meet.

The structure of theses and dissertations

Recent years have seen increased attention being given to thesis and dissertation writing in the literature on teaching English for specific purposes. Clearly, though, a thesis or dissertation is more than its organizational structure. Equally, there are many factors which influence decisions a student makes about the form of their text. These include the research perspective taken in the study, the purpose of the text, and the extent to which the student has been given advice on the positioning and organization of their text (Prior 1995).

The form of the thesis or dissertation is also influenced by the values and expectations of the academic discipline in which it is produced and will be assessed. The structure of a text is, nevertheless, a central issue in text processing and production (Johns 1995) and one which is important for students to have an awareness of so they can make choices from the range of patterns of textual organization that are typically associated with instances of the particular genre.

A number of researchers have discussed the organization of different thesis types. Dudley-Evans (1999) terms the typical 'IMRAD' (introduction–methods–results–discussion) type thesis a 'traditional' thesis. Thompson (1999) further refines this category by dividing traditional theses into those which have 'simple' and those which have 'complex' patterns of organization. A thesis with a 'simple' traditional pattern is one which reports on a single study and has a typical organizational structure of 'introduction', 'review of the literature', 'materials and methods', 'results', 'discussion' and 'conclusion'. The table of contents of a typical 'simple' traditional thesis is shown in Box 5.1 (on p.68). This thesis is an examination of rater consistency in the assessment of second-language writing.

A thesis with a 'complex' internal structure is one that reports on more than one study. It typically commences with 'introduction' and 'review of the literature' sections, as with the simple traditional thesis. It might then have a 'general methods' section which is followed by a series of sections that report on each of the individual studies. The thesis ends with a general overall conclusions section (Thompson 1999).

Box 5.1 A 'simple' traditional thesis

Degree: MEd   *Study area:* Education
Title: Rater consistency and judgment in the direct assessment of second-language writing ability

Chapter 1: Introduction
The nature of the problem
Origins of the study
Focus and structure of the thesis

Chapter 2: Literature review
Introduction
Performance assessment
Performance assessment and reliability
Conclusion

Chapter 3: Methodology
Introduction
Selection of research design, setting, informants and texts
Data collection and analysis
Conclusion

Chapter 4: Results
Introduction
Degree of rater consistency
Interpretation and application of performance criteria
Raters' reading strategies
Influences on rater judgments of writing ability
Conclusion

Chapter 5: Discussion
Introduction
Degree of rater consistency
Interpretation and application of performance criteria
Raters' reading strategies
Influences on rater judgments of writing ability
Conclusion

Chapter 6: Conclusions and recommendations
Source: Paltridge 2002: 138–139

A sample 'complex' traditional thesis is shown in Box 5.2. The thesis reports on community perceptions of the notion of town character in a small coastal town in Australia. Even though the thesis is titled 'a case study', it actually reports on a number of case studies (five in all), each related to its overall topic. The thesis starts with a general introductory chapter which presents

Box 5.2 A 'complex' traditional thesis

Degree: PhD   *Study area:* Architecture, building and planning
Title: Community perceptions of town character: a case study of Byron Bay

Chapter 1: Introduction
The concept of town character
Research strategy
Thesis structure

Chapter 2: Byron Bay: from sacred site to tourist attraction
Regional setting, natural history and cultural history
Concern with maintaining town character

Chapter 3: Place character: a theoretical framework
Spirit and concept of place
Models of place
Dimensions of place character

Chapter 4: Methodological considerations
Community involvement in assessing town character
Landscape assessment paradigms and methods
Research design

Chapter 5: A threat to town character
Club Med development proposal
Research questions
Method
Results
Conclusions
Limitations and future research

Chapter 6: Community description of town character
Survey aims and research questions
Method
Results
Discussion

Chapter 7: Identifying town character features
Research questions
Method
Results
Discussion

Chapter 8: Relating landscape features to town character
Research questions
Inventory of town character features
Randomly selected landscape scenes
Part One: respondents, and rating scales
Analysis and results
Part Two: respondents and rating scales
Analysis and results
Discussion and further research
Conclusion

Chapter 9: General discussion
Addressing the research questions
Concluding remarks

Source: Paltridge 2002: 139–140

key notions relevant to the study, a general description of the research strategy employed, and an overview of the thesis. This is followed by two chapters which provide further background to the study. The five case studies are then presented. The thesis concludes with a general discussion chapter which draws the findings of the study together and makes suggestions for future application of the findings, as well as discussing limitations to these findings.

Dudley-Evans (1999) refers to a further kind of thesis, which he terms a 'topic-based' thesis. This kind of thesis typically commences with an introductory chapter which is then followed by a series of chapters that have titles based on sub-topics of the topic under investigation. The thesis then ends with a 'conclusions' chapter. The PhD thesis he reports on, written in the field of electronic engineering, is made up of nine chapters, seven of which are topic based. The example of a topic-based master's thesis shown in Box 5.3 was written in the area of cultural studies. It examines pink and white marble terraces in New Zealand which were covered by volcanic eruption in the late 1800s and are now an historical and 'museumised' tourist attraction.

Dong (1998) describes doctoral theses which are based on a compilation of publishable research articles. These are quite different from other sorts of theses. The research article chapters are more concise than typical thesis chapters, with less of the 'display of knowledge' that is often found in a thesis or dissertation. Further, in terms of audience, they are written more as 'experts writing for experts', than novices 'writing for admission to the academy'. In this sense, they are quite different from the 'traditional: complex' type thesis described above. Dong found that 38 per cent of the graduate students at the two US universities where she carried out her study were writing a thesis based on publishable

---

Box 5.3 A topic-based thesis

Degree: MA   *Study area:* Cultural studies
Title: Unworldly places: Myth, memory and the Pink and White Terraces

Chapter 1: Introduction
Disappearing wonders

Chapter 2: Plotting
Travels of colonial science
Plotting destinations

Chapter 3: Sightseeing
Topophilic tourism
Site specifics
Painting the place and myth
Souvenering the site

Chapter 4: Astral travel
Mnemonic tours in the 'new wonderland'
Memory tours
The buried village: Embalmed history
Living out the past
Museumising the past: Sanctioned memory

Chapter 5: Postscript

Source: Paltridge 2002: 140

---

research articles, although native-speaker students tended to be doing this more than second-language students. She found, however, that this type of thesis was more common at one of the universities, a comprehensive research university, than at the other, a technical and engineering university. The compilation of research articles presented for the PhD in dental science summarized in Box 5.4 (on p. 72) is very similar to the type of thesis Dong (1998) reports is now common in science PhDs in the United States. This thesis was based on three discrete but related research articles, one of which had already been published at the time of submission and was included as an appendix to the thesis.

A study carried out by Paltridge (2002) found that more than half the theses written in the collection of texts he examined at his university were traditional in their format and reported on a single study; that is, they represented the 'traditional: simple' kind of thesis. Nonetheless, a good number of theses did not follow this pattern. There were, for example, equal numbers of 'traditional: complex' type theses and 'topic-based' theses. Further, there was one thesis in the collection of texts he examined which was made up of a collection of research articles, each presented as an individual chapter and framed by a number of introductory and concluding chapters.

Box 5.4 A compilation of research articles presented as a PhD thesis

Degree: PhD   *Study area:* Dental science
Title: Vertical root fracture and fracture-related properties of dentine

Chapter 1: Introduction

Chapter 2: Background and literature review

Chapter 3: Aims of the study

Chapter 4: Load and strain during lateral condensation and vertical root fracture
Introduction
Literature review
Materials and methods
Results
Discussion
Summary and conclusions

Chapter 5: Mechanism of vertical root fracture by finite element analysis and strain gauge technique
Introduction
Literature review
Materials and methods
Results
Discussion
Summary and conclusions

Chapter 6: The effects of dentine location and tubule orientation on selected physical properties of dentine
Introduction
Literature review
Materials and methods
Results
Discussion
Summary and conclusions

Chapter 7: Additional finite element analysis and general discussion

Chapter 8: Further work and investigations

Source: Paltridge 2002: 140

Box 5.5 is a summary of the thesis types found in this study and their typical structure. This is presented in very general terms as a statement of what typically occurs in each of these thesis types. Sections in brackets indicate that they occurred in some of the theses but not in all of them. In a way, both the 'traditional: complex' and compilations of research articles are a variation of

Box 5.5 Summary of thesis types and their typical organizational structures

Traditional: simple
Introduction
Literature review
Materials and methods
Results
Discussion
Conclusions

Traditional: complex
Introduction
Background to the study and review
of the literature
(Background theory)
(General methods)
Study 1
    Introduction
    Methods
    Results
    Discussion and conclusions
Study 2
    Introduction
    Methods
    Results
    Discussion and conclusions
Study 3 etc
    Introduction
    Methods
    Results
    Discussion and conclusions
Discussion
Conclusions

Topic-based
Introduction
Topic 1
Topic 2
Topic 3 etc
Conclusions

Compilation of research articles
Introduction
Background to the study

Research article 1
  Introduction
  Literature review
  Materials and methods
  Results
  Discussion
  Conclusions
Research article 2
  Introduction
  Literature review
  Materials and methods
  Results
  Discussion
  Conclusions
Research article 3 etc
  Introduction
  Literature review
  Materials and methods
  Results
  Discussion
  Conclusions
Discussion
Conclusions

Source: Paltridge 2002: 130

the 'traditional: simple' type thesis. One difference between these two types of thesis, however, seems to be the place of the review of the literature which is presented in more detail and earlier on in the 'traditional: complex' type thesis and more within each of the articles in the compilation type format. The research article chapters of the compilation type thesis are also much more 'stand alone' than the individual study chapters of the 'traditional: complex' type thesis. Also the intended audience, level of detail and display of knowledge presented in these two types of thesis, as mentioned above, are substantially different. The topic-based format is, however, of a very different kind. Often, these types of thesis do not have what might be considered a materials and methods type section and often do not have separate results and discussion sections. Starfield and Ravelli (2006) found in their study of humanities and social science theses that the majority of the theses they looked at (18 out of 20) were of this kind.

All of this may seem somewhat unremarkable to someone who has read or supervised many theses or dissertations. Few second-language students embarking on thesis and dissertation writing are likely to have seen many of these kinds of texts before they start writing. Thus, what to experienced researchers and supervisors might seem common knowledge, to a great number of their students, perhaps, is not.

Application: thesis types

Ask your student to look at the summary of thesis types shown in Box 5.5. Which of these would most suit their thesis? Why?

Analysing sample theses and dissertations

It is useful for students to look at a range of sample texts as possible models for their pieces of writing. One helpful way of doing this is to ask students to choose a thesis with a topic and research perspective which is similar in some way to their own and to use for their own 'online' genre analysis (Flowerdew 1993) of the text. In some universities, academic departments keep copies of theses and dissertations that have been submitted in their area of study. These copies are often easier to access than centrally held ones and are thus a better starting point for students than those held in the university's main libraries. Completed theses and dissertations are also available via a number of online services (see Chapter 12). Students can be asked to identify the typical macro-structure of the kind of thesis they are preparing to write. They can be asked to examine the way their sample text is divided up into stages, as well as consider the function each of these stages performs in achieving its overall goal.

Application: sections of a thesis

Ask your student to find a thesis in their university library with a similar research perspective to their own. Ask them to examine the way the thesis is divided up into sections, as well as considering the function each of these sections performs in the overall goal of the thesis.

The content of individual chapters

The content of individual chapters is discussed in detail in the chapters that follow. Box 5.6 (on p. 76) is a summary of the 'traditional structure' for writing up a thesis or dissertation and the content that typically occurs in each of these chapters. For a PhD there may be more chapters than this, depending on how the study was carried out, but it will most likely, if it is 'traditional' in some way, follow this kind of organization, or some sort of variation of it.

Box 5.6 Typical content of individual chapters

Chapter 1: Introduction
General background information on the project
The research problem
Purpose of the study
Hypotheses or research questions
Scope of the study
Significance of the study
Definitions of key terms
Organization of the thesis

Chapter 2: Literature review
General review of relevant literature
Specific topics directly relating to the issue under investigation
How previous research suggests the study is important to do
The gap in the research that the study will fill

Chapter 3: Conceptual framework and/or methodology
Research design
Methods used to collect data
Research instruments
Methods used to analyse the data
Details about who, how, when and why
For ethnography, description of the setting and participants
Issues of ethics and consent

Chapter 4: Results
The findings of the study, described under themes that emerged from the data, under the research questions or under the data collection techniques that were used

Chapter 5: Discussion and conclusions
A re-statement of the research problem
A re-statement of results
Discussion of what was found in relation to previous research on the topic
Limitations of the study
Implications for future research
Consent

Writing chapter outlines

Moore and Searcy's (1998) 'Theses and dissertations: a guided tour' provides many useful suggestions for students to analyse sample dissertations in preparation for planning the organization of their own theses and dissertations. In this activity, students analyse a dissertation with a similar research perspective to their own to identify its organizational structure. This analysis takes them through the major sections of their sample dissertation, considering both the content and organization of the stages of the text as they go. They are then asked to consider the reasons for the various organizational choices the writers of their texts have made. Students then use the results of their analyses as a guide for preparing the writing of their dissertations. This use of models not only gives students a guide to conventional forms of texts (Dudley-Evans 1997), but also provides 'valuable clues to the status of knowledge in the field' (Charney and Carlson 1995: 116). The activity in the following Application is based on Moore and Searcy's (1998) guidelines.

Application: tables of contents (i)

Ask your student to look at a sample thesis in their area of study which has a similar research perspective to their own and answer the following set of questions:

(a) How many sections is the thesis divided into? Is a numbering system used for sections and subsections? How many levels are there (e.g. 1.5.2 = three levels)?

(b) Which sections are included before the introduction (e.g. abstract, acknowledgements, etc.)? How are these set apart from the main sections of the thesis (e.g. with Roman numerals)?

Application: tables of contents (ii)

Ask your student to prepare a sample table of contents for their thesis, using the thesis they examined as a starting point and list of chapter contents shown above. Ask them to bring it to you and explain why they organized it in the way they did.

Linking sections

A typical feature of thesis and dissertation writing is the way in which sections of the text are connected by the use of linking sections. This is often done through the use of what Mauranen (1993) calls *metatext*, or text that 'talks about the text'. The following example, from the Introduction to a PhD thesis in applied linguistics, is typical of the kind of metatext found in theses and dissertations. The thesis is an analysis of scientific writing. Every sentence in this extract is text that is 'talking about the text'.

> This chapter has presented the background to the study which will be described in the chapters which follow. It has examined the concepts of genre and English for Specific Purposes as well as described and provided examples of a number of approaches to genre analysis. It has also provided arguments in support of the concept of genre as an organizing principle for language programme development. It has outlined the purpose and design of the study, including a brief discussion of the process of selection and analysis of the texts used. The chapter which follows will present the theoretical framework for the study.

Application: metatext

Ask your student to look at their sample thesis for examples of the kind of metatext described above. In what other ways do thesis writers 'talk about their text'?

Bunton (1999) discusses further ways in which thesis and dissertation writers talk about the organization of their texts. He groups these as *previews*, *overviews* and *reviews*. Previews look forward in the text: they anticipate what will come in the text, and may summarize or refer to a later stage of the text. A preview may refer to the thesis as a whole, a chapter, a section of the text, a paragraph or a sentence in the text. The following, from the previous extract, is an example of a preview which refers to a chapter that is yet to come in the text: 'The chapter which follows will present the theoretical framework for the study'.

Overviews may look in both directions, forward or backward in the text. They may also refer to the current stage of the text, in overall terms. They may refer to a whole chapter or a section of the text. The following is an example of an overview. It describes the contents of the present chapter, in overall terms.

> The purpose of this chapter has been to test the findings of the first stage of the study as well as submit the texts analysed in the first stage of the study to a contrasting analytic perspective. It has also presented an analysis of a number of specific purpose texts as a demonstration of how the framework described in Chapter 4 can be applied to provide an explanation of genre assignment. This chapter has also investigated the relationship between frames and language. Finally, it has reached a number of conclusions based on this further stage of the study.

Reviews look back, repeat, summarize or refer to an earlier stage of the text. The following example, from the second chapter of a thesis on barrister–client interactions, is an example of a review. It is then followed by a preview.

> The previous chapter of this study described the background to the study, including reference to other research in legal settings. It also described the aspects of conversation analysis which will be drawn on for this study. Those aspects of investigation, further, were placed within an ethnomethodological framework. The chapter also described the focus of the research and its conceptual framework. Finally it defined the scope, design and limitations of the study and the concepts and terminology employed.
>
> This chapter presents information relating to the method of data collection and analysis of that data. It describes the physical setting of the interactions, the participants in the interactions and, further, the purpose of the interaction.
>
> (O'Shannessy 1995: 19)

Application: previews, overviews and reviews

Ask your student to look at their sample thesis for examples of the kind of previews, overviews and reviews described above. Ask them to think about how putting these in their text could 'help their reader' through their text.

Overview of the thesis

A further example of metatext often occurs in the first chapter of a thesis where the writer has a section titled 'Overview of the thesis' (or 'Overview of the study', etc.). This section is, at the same time, an example of a preview, an overview and a review. Thesis writers include this section to help their reader through their text; that is, as a way of signalling where the thesis is going and where they can expect to find key information about their project. As Manalo and Trafford (2004: 93) point out, a thesis 'is not a mystery novel'. Students need to provide a clear 'road map' for their thesis 'explaining what it contains and where those contents can be found' (see Chapter 6 for further discussion of this).

Discipline-specific expectations

While there are general expectations of thesis and dissertation writing (see Chapter 1), there are also discipline-specific expectations for thesis and dissertation organization. Many of these disciplinary conventions and expectations, however, are subtle. As Parry (1998: 273) argues:

> [these conventions] may not be readily identifiable to experienced schol-
> ars, yet doctoral students are expected to learn and master them,
> suggesting that discipline specific writing norms and conventions are
> learned largely by tacit means during doctoral study.

One of the arguments this book is making is that the more these norms and
conventions can be made explicit, the better (and more easily) students will be
able to learn them. The Application activities in this book have just this goal.

Among the discipline-specific conventions listed by Parry are the structure of academic argument, the ways in which ideas are linked in a text, and
conventions for citation and critique. Different disciplines also often have
their own preferred ways of doing things in terms of thesis organization. It
is important to make these as explicit as possible for students. This may
vary, of course, depending on the type of thesis being written and the
research perspective being taken by the student. Writers such as Belcher
and Hirvela (2005) have argued that the qualitative thesis, for example, is
in many ways 'a fuzzy genre' (Medway 2002). That is, there is often more
variation in a qualitative thesis than in a quantitative thesis in terms of how
it should be written, the issues it should address, the claims it can make and
how it can do this (see Chapter 8 for further discussion of this). The qualitative thesis is also often more difficult for second-language students to
write (Belcher and Hirvela 2005).

Application: discipline-specific expectations

Ask your student to look at a number of theses or dissertations written
in their area of study to identify discipline-specific expectations for
organizing their thesis or dissertation. Ask them to make a list of these
and bring them to you for discussion.

Conclusion

Thinking about the shape and organization of the thesis or dissertation, and
various ways of organizing tables of contents, may seem like a somewhat technical affair to be discussing with students. The table of contents may be the
last thing a student writes, but is often one of the first things an examiner
will read. The table of contents along with the thesis title are important 'sites
of identity negotiation where the writer begins to align him or herself with a
research tradition' (Starfield and Ravelli 2006: 226). The contents pages present an overview of the thesis and, as such, act as an initial guide for the
reader of thesis. They also start to show how the student has located their
work within a particular disciplinary, and research, culture. As Starfield and
Ravelli (2006: 226) observe:

all the reading, research and writing the candidate has undertaken ... begins to be presented in the contents pages, for the reader (examiner) to recognize, and accept or reject as a valid contribution to a research culture.

Chapter 6

Writing the Introduction

The introductory chapter

Bunton (2002) and Paltridge (2002) found that despite variation in the overall structuring of the thesis with the emergence of new 'hybrid' types (see Chapter 5), all the theses they examined had an introductory chapter. Our understandings of the structure and organization of the Introductions to theses draw on the research into journal article Introductions, primarily carried out by Swales (1990). Readers may be familiar with his Create a Research Space (CARS) framework. Introductory chapters have in fact probably been subjected to greater examination than other typical sections of the thesis genre (Bunton 2002; Dudley-Evans 1986). This may be because they are themselves shorter and therefore more amenable to analysis than the other typically much longer sections, but whatever the cause, there is more research upon which to draw when we look at thesis Introductions. This allows us to propose a framework for the typical structure of thesis Introductions (see Table 6.1).

As Swales and Feak (1994) have argued in terms of the research article, the thesis Introduction is of strategic importance: its key role is to create a research space for the writer. It is in the Introduction that the writer makes claims for the centrality or significance of the research in question and begins to outline the overall argument of the thesis. In the fierce academic competition to get papers published in reputable academic journals, the Introduction is extremely important in positioning the writer as having something to say that is worth publishing. This is not as true for the thesis writer who is seeking to enter a community of scholars but as Bunton (2002: 58) notes, 'since one of the criteria for the award of a doctorate in many universities is that the thesis makes an original contribution of knowledge', the doctoral student needs to establish in the Introduction how the thesis relates to and builds upon previous research in the field (see Chapter 4 on research proposals). In a study carried out in Hong Kong, Allison *et al.* (1998: 212) found that 'failure to create a "research space"' was a key shortcoming in the thesis writing of the non-native speakers of English at their university.

Table 6.1 Typical moves in thesis Introductions

Move 1	Establishing a research territory
	a by showing that the general research area is important, central, interesting, problematic, or relevant in some way (optional)
	b by providing background information about the topic (optional)
	c by introducing and reviewing items of previous research in the area (obligatory)
	d by defining terms (optional)
Move 2	Establishing a niche
	a by indicating a gap in the previous research, raising a question about it, or extending previous knowledge in some way (obligatory)
	b by identifying a problem/need (optional)
Move 3	Occupying the niche
	a by outlining purposes/aims, or stating the nature of the present research or research questions/hypotheses (obligatory)
	b by announcing principal findings/stating value of research (optional)
	c by indicating the structure of the thesis and providing mini-synopses (previews) of each subsequent chapter (obligatory)
	d by outlining the theoretical position (optional)
	e by describing the methods used in the study (optional)

Source: based on Swales and Feak 1994: 175 and Bunton 2002: 67

This chapter discusses the role of the Introduction in relation to the thesis as a whole, the typical structure of the Introduction and some of the linguistic characteristics of thesis Introductions. Examples of Introductions from a science thesis and a social science thesis are examined in terms of the proposed framework and suggestions for supervisors provided.

The role of the introductory chapter in the thesis: creating a research space

We have found that despite the growing variation in thesis structure and organization at the macro-level, it is useful to begin by considering the role of the Introduction in relation to the thesis in its entirety. The thesis is said to be shaped like an hourglass that is open at the top and bottom (see Figure 6.1 on p.84). The Introduction sits in the upper open end of the hourglass bowl to indicate that it is in the Introduction that the researcher clearly signals the relationship between the specific topic of the thesis and the field of work into which the thesis is being inserted.

Chapter 4 (on writing research proposals) illustrated the importance of situating the proposed research in relation to a field of inquiry. This is, in large part, the role of the introductory chapter. As all our work in some way talks to previous work and develops upon it, the top of the hourglass is open and the 'bulb' of the glass is broad. As the thesis develops to focus on the specific topic of the research and the particular methodology employed, the

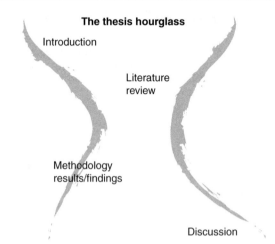

Figure 6.1 The thesis hourglass
Source: adapted from Atkinson and Curtis 1998: 52

hourglass narrows, only to broaden out when the findings/results are examined and then discussed in terms of how they add to the body of existing knowledge in the field. Whereas in many journal articles the introductory section will contain a review of the relevant literature, in the thesis, the literature is almost always reviewed in a separate chapter or sometimes in more than one chapter. This is in fact one of the distinguishing characteristics of the thesis as its length allows for the development of an extensive literature review and explicit theoretical framework. It is particularly important for the thesis writer, who is both a student and a novice member of the research community, to locate his/her work adequately in relation to the field and acknowledge their intellectual 'debts' explicitly. The Introduction, nonetheless, typically reviews some of the key literature in the field in order to situate the research.

Only two of the 20 PhD thesis Introductions examined by Starfield and Ravelli (2006) were numbered Chapter 1. The other 18 were therefore located outside the numbering system and preceded the first chapter – underlining the overview function of the Introduction and how important it is for the student writer to preview the entire thesis structure in their introductory chapter.

How long should the Introduction be?

Typically, the introductory chapter is one of the shorter chapters of the entire thesis. The 45 thesis Introductions examined by Bunton (2002) averaged 17.4 pages in length with a good deal of disciplinary variation. He found that Introductions from medicine were particularly long (29–45 pages) and that this was because they included the substantial review of the literature. Where social sciences and arts Introductions did this, they were also over 40 pages in length. It appears, both from Bunton's (2002) research and our own observations, that certain humanities' (arts) theses may not have separate literature review chapters but that a review of the literature is conducted in the introductory chapter. However, 32 of the Introductions examined by Bunton did not have more references to the literature than any other of the thesis chapters. This finding underlines one of the key differences between the research article and the thesis mentioned above – the almost obligatory separate literature review chapter.

Application

One of the key aims of this section of our book is to help student and supervisor develop a shared and accessible language for talking about thesis writing to assist in raising awareness of the typical generic structure of the thesis. Our experience is that this is empowering for both supervisor and student.

- Ask your student to draw up a plan showing how their thesis would or would not fit into the hourglass framework. If it does not fit into the framework, ask them to explain why.
- Show your student some examples of recent theses from your field and ask them to assess the extent to which the 'hourglass' appears to have been followed. We find it important to stress to students that they do have choices in how they shape their theses.
- Ask them to note whether the Introduction is 'Chapter 1' or stands outside the chapter numbering system. If it is not Chapter 1, ask them to reflect on why this might be so.
- Ask students if they would like to use the same chapter titles as in the thesis hourglass, or not. If not, ask them to explain why. We are finding that in the humanities, in particular, and to some extent in the social sciences, many thesis chapters do not have easily identifiable 'literature review' or 'methodology' chapters. Rather, chapters tend to have catchy, evocative titles which refer to thesis themes.
- Focus in particular on the role of the Introduction. Remind them that all theses have introductory chapters. Introduce the notion of creating a research space. Link this to the criteria for assessing a PhD, one of which is a significant contribution to knowledge in the chosen field. The establishment of a niche or gap in the research territory is therefore crucial for the student.
- Ask students to write a few sentences describing the 'gap' their study will fill.

- Briefly discuss differences between research article Introductions and thesis Introductions as students will be more familiar with journal articles. Then ask students to examine a research article and a thesis on a similar topic in their area of study and draw up a list of similarities and differences in the Introductions to each of them.

The typical structure of the Introduction

As we said earlier, recent research has provided a more detailed understanding of the generic structure of thesis Introductions (Bunton 2002; Dudley-Evans 1986). The organizational structure of the Introduction can be said to move from a fairly general overview of the research terrain to the particular issues under investigation through three key moves which capture the communicative purposes of the Introduction (Swales and Feak 1994):

- to establish a research territory;
- to identify a niche or gap in the territory;
- to then signal how the topic in question occupies that niche.

Table 6.1 is a modified version of Swales and Feak's move structure (drawing on Bunton 2002) which can usefully be applied to introductory chapters. In Table 6.1, the sub-moves (indicated by lower case a, b, etc.) have been elaborated on. It is important to note that not all sub-moves will necessarily be found: these are labelled optional.

In Move 1 – *establishing a research territory* – the writer typically begins to carve out his/her own research space by indicating that the general area is in some way significant. This is often done through reviewing previous research in the field. In addition, the writer may choose to provide background information on the particular topic being investigated and may define key terms which are essential for the study.

The different moves in the Introduction tend to employ different tenses (Atkinson and Curtis 1998). Move 1a, which signals the importance of the general area of research, often uses verbs in either the present tense or the present perfect tense in the sentence which makes these claims to *centrality* (Swales and Feak 1994). In the extracts below, the verbs in the present or present perfect tenses of sentences taken from Move 1a of a selection of PhD theses are underlined. The writer's use of the present tense suggests that the statement is a generally accepted truth. The use of the present perfect tense (i.e. has been) in the third sentence functions similarly to describe a state that continues up to the present moment. This sub-move also often contains an adjective, shown below in italics, which emphasizes the importance or interest of the topic.

- In these areas, reducing groundwater recharge <u>is</u> an *important* step in reducing land degradation caused by salinity (Lewis 2000: 1).
- The Magellanic Clouds <u>provide</u> a *unique* environment in which to study *many interesting* and astrophysically *challenging* problems (Amy 2000: 1).
- Speech <u>has</u> arguably <u>been</u> the *most important* form of human communication since languages were first conceived (Epps 2000: 1).
- The modeling of fluid flows <u>is</u> of *great interest* to Engineers and Scientists alike, with many engineering problems and issues of scientific interest depending upon complex flow phenomena (Norris 2000: 1).

Move 2 – *establishing a niche* – points to a 'gap' or niche in the previous research which the research will 'fill'. For Swales and Feak (1994), the metaphor of the niche or research space is based on the idea of competition in ecology – academic writers seeking to publish must compete for 'light and space' as do plants and animals. Elsewhere, when describing writing a conference abstract, Swales and Feak (2000) use a marketing metaphor to talk about 'selling' one's research, and the niche metaphor can be extended to the notion of niche marketing – identifying a specific gap in the market which the new product can fill. While comparing one's thesis to a marketable product may initially appear distasteful, we have found it useful to talk in these terms to our students; the dissertation must after all make an original contribution to the field. The market niche metaphor is also helpful in understanding the idea of the Introduction as enabling the writer to position themselves in the marketplace of ideas relative to what has been written by others in the field. In the thesis, the gap is also sometimes presented as a problem or need that has been identified as requiring further research.

In Move 2 of the framework, the writer typically establishes a niche by indicating a gap in the previous research or possibly extending a current research approach into a new area. It is through the review of prior research that the gap is established. The language of 'gap statements', according to Atkinson and Curtis (1998: 63), is typically evaluative in a negative way. In the examples listed below, gap statements from the Introductions of master's and doctoral theses have the gap words and phrases in italics.

- One class of quality improvement which has *not received much attention* is enhancement by broadening the bandwidth of coded speech without an increase in the bit rate. This is surprising since the notion of quality as a function of speech bandwidth is anticipated to become more pervasive (Epps 2000: 4).
- Due to the complexity of the flow problems *there are few* analytic models of fluid flows, but the advent of digital computers has stimulated the development of numerical method for the modeling of flow (Norris 2000: 1).

- Indeed, there appeared to be a story of female agitation for Aboriginal rights in twentieth century Australia that *had largely gone unnoticed up to that point*, and in the context of contemporary feminist politics *was positively denied* (Holland 1998: 1).
- Although it became accepted that episodic recharge might be a factor in the agricultural areas of Western Australia (e.g. Nulsen 1993), *no systematic analyses of* where and when it occurred, and how important it was in the overall picture of groundwater recharge and salinity were carried out (Lewis 2000: 6).
- These observations point to the proposition that in order to recognize the mismatches and to begin to understand the consequences of discontinuities, *there is a need to increase* research knowledge of community social practices and interactions with community literacies (White-Davison 1999: 2).
- *It is important to take issue with* his criticism of the role of structuralism and post-structuralism (Wakeling 1998: 5).

The lists below, from Swales and Feak (1994: 187–189), contain examples of typical 'gap statement' words and phrases which may be useful for the non-native English speaker.

Verbs

disregard	neglect to consider
fail to consider	overestimate
ignore	overlook
is limited to	suffer from
misinterpret	underestimate

Adjectives

controversial	questionable
incomplete	unconvincing
inconclusive	unsatisfactory
misguided	

Noun phrase

Little information/attention/work/data/research
Few studies/investigations/researchers/attempts
No studies/data/calculations
None of these studies/findings/calculations

Other forms

However
It remains unclear
It would be of interest to

As Swales and Feak (1994) point out, language which identifies weaknesses in the writing of others needs to be used with care. This is particularly the case for thesis writers, who are students seeking to be accepted into a community of scholars.

In Move 3 – *occupying the niche* – the writer, by outlining the purposes of their own research, indicates to the reader how the proposed research will 'fill' the identified niche or gap. In a thesis, the principal findings will frequently be previewed and theoretical positions as well as methods used may be outlined. It is here that the writer can signal the value or significance of the research (Move 3b). However, Move 3c, in which the overall structure of the thesis is previewed, including a mini-synopsis of each chapter, is considered obligatory.

This sub-move (3c) typically contains much metadiscourse. Metadiscourse (also referred to as metatext) refers to discourse about discourse; how writers talk about their writing and the structure of their writing, when they are not talking about the content of their writing (Bunton 1999; Vande Kopple 1985). In extended texts such as theses, metadiscourse plays an important role in that it helps provide an overarching organizational scaffold for the thesis, and guides readers (that is, the examiners) through the text, by frequent forward and backward references and overviews. In fact, one of the significant differences that has been identified between the journal article and the thesis is in the greater use made of metadiscourse in the much lengthier thesis (Swales 1990).

Examples of metadiscourse are phrases such as 'Chapter 2 examines'; 'this thesis argues that'; 'the following section reviews'. Metadiscourse in the Introduction is likely to take the form of forward reference to what is still to come and to the overall structure of the thesis (Move 3c of our framework) but may also be found in the writer's development of the central argument of the thesis. According to Bunton (1999), it is metadiscourse that refers to chapters or to the thesis as a whole that is distinctive to the dissertation, as this type of metadiscourse would not be found in a journal article. Bunton examined the ways in which 13 PhD theses by Hong Kong research students used metadiscourse to 'orient and guide their readers' through their theses. All but one of the theses previewed the entire thesis in their Introductions; that is, referred to the thesis itself with expressions such as, 'the focus of this thesis is on'; 'the plan for this thesis is' (Bunton 1999: S48). However, only eight of the 13 previewed each subsequent chapter. Bunton's findings suggest that non-native speakers of English may need to be encouraged to make greater use of previewing strategies in their theses as a whole and specifically in their Introductions where they should be encouraged to preview each of the subsequent chapters.

Much typical thesis metadiscourse is found in the language of Move 3 of our framework: where the writer signals their 'occupation' of the niche established in Move 2. The move will often begin with nouns that refer to the thesis or to the research itself and will use verbs that refer to the research process, particularly as the various chapters of the thesis are previewed. A sentence beginning 'This thesis/study …' can be followed by any of the following verbs (and others not listed) depending on the emphasis the writer wishes to place or to vary the language used: describes; develops; studies; discusses; examines; introduces; aims (to); reports; explores; shows; focuses; presents (adapted from Atkinson and Curtis 1998: 65). The verbs tend to be in the present tense as this makes the research seems relevant and current (see Swales and Feak 1994).

Box 6.1 shows Move 3c – *outline of following chapters* – from a master's thesis (White-Davison 1999). Words or phrases which refer to the thesis itself and which function to preview later stages of the thesis are in italics, as are verbs which refer to the research process.

Box 6.1 Language patterns in Move 3c

Outline of the chapters

This chapter has provided the background to *this study* and *the study's* objectives, and placed these within the context of the large project that was conducted in 1993–1994.

Chapter 2 provides a theoretical and empirical framework for the study *by reviewing* current literature on rurality and rural living, and on communities and schooling and cultural practices. Literature pertaining to methodology for qualitative research, specifically on ethnomethodology, and methods of interview analysis and the application of these methods *is also reviewed* in *Chapter 2*.

Chapter 3 explains the methods that have been used for conducting the research and for the analysis of the data used in this study. *It describes the study* sites and participants, the operational procedures used for the large project and for *this study*, the instruments for data collection, the selection of data for analysis, and the methods of interview analysis for *this study*.

Chapters 4 and 5 present the results of interview analysis based on a selection of themes, and provide discussion of these themes and the issues raised. *Chapter 4 reports* results of interview analysis on the themes of community living and lifestyle choice, and the culture of rural communities. *It gives some insights* into the views of rural residents on their choice of lifestyle and rural living, and their views on the importance of cultural identity. *Chapter 5 reports* results of interview analysis on the themes of schooling in rural communities, rural residents' views of the relationships between various kinds of work and education, the community's culture and schooling, and gendered roles in rural communities.

Chapter 6 summarises the research findings, draws conclusions from *those findings,* and *indicates* some of the implications of *the findings.* Limitations of the study and suggestions for further research in this field *are considered.*

Source: White-Davison 1999

It is through the use of these three moves, often in a cyclical manner, that the writer justifies the relevance of his/her own research. The moves are not necessarily found in linear order and may be recycled several times over the course of the Introduction (Bunton 2002). Bunton's (2002: 65) study found that all but one of the 45 Introductions analysed contained 'sequences of text' which corresponded to the three moves in Swales' structure of research article introductions. In the vast majority of the Introductions he looked at, the typical organizational pattern consisted of Move 1 (establishing a research territory), followed by Move 2 (establishing a niche), with this pattern being recycled several times. Move 3 (occupying the niche) typically appeared only towards the end of the Introduction as the writers introduced their own research after having reviewed the literature and pointed to gaps or problems as they did so.

Thesis Introductions from a range of fields would seem to follow the basic move structure. Where the thesis differs from the research article is in its length and in the possible recycling of the moves as the writer examines various aspects of the research. In no sense, however, is this framework a formula to be unthinkingly applied. While the moves may not always be found, or found in the sequence suggested, they are typically found and provide students and their supervisors with a set of useful tools for analysing introductory chapters and for thinking about their potential structure. There is indeed a sense in which both this framework and the hourglass shape – the visual shape of the thesis – embody in essence much of the communicative purpose of the thesis.

In Box 6.2 (on p.92), the framework is applied to the explicitly entitled *overview* section, extracted from the beginning of the Introduction to a PhD thesis in physics (Amy 2000). Moves and sub-moves are identified and labelled. Words that signal the significance of the topic are underlined, as are gap words and phrases. Move 3c does not appear in full in this extract but towards the end of the thesis chapter.

Box 6.2 Extract from Introduction of a PhD thesis in physics

Chapter 1
Introduction
1.1 Overview

Claiming
centrality

The Magellanic Clouds provide a unique environment in which
to study many *interesting* and astrophysically *challenging* problems. 1a
They are relatively nearby, have a position which makes them
observable for the entire year and they provide *ideal* case studies to
investigate many classes of sources. Although distances to both the
Small and Large Magellanic Clouds are still somewhat uncertain, 1b
they are relatively well-known, allowing detailed quantitative
studies to be undertaken. The Clouds have been studied over a wide
range of frequencies, from low-frequency radio observations
through to satellite based gamma-ray studies.

Establishing
a research
territory

The Magellanic Clouds are one of the prime observing targets for
the Molonglo Observatory Synthesis Telescope (MOST). Soon after
the instrument was commissioned in 1981 an observing programme
to survey both the Small and Large Magellanic Clouds was
undertaken. Operating at a frequency of 843 MHz with an angular 1b
resolution of 44 arcsec, the MOST was the highest angular
resolution aperture synthesis radio telescope in the southern
hemisphere in regular use at that time. The resulting sub-arcminute
angular resolution images provide an excellent base from which to
select objects for further study. The MOST Magellanic Cloud surveys
were in progress when the work reported here was started and the
images from the MOST Small Magellanic Cloud survey have since 1c
been published in Turtle *et al.* (1998).

Indicating
a gap

The MOST is a powerful imaging instrument particularly suited to
radio surveys and to imaging, in a single 12-hour observation, 1d
sources with complex extended morphologies. In addition to 'full
synthesis' observations, an observing mode called 'CUTS' can be
used in which around 10 sources are each observed for a few minutes
with a cadence of approximately one hour over the course of an
observation. In this way a number of sources can be imaged in a
single observing session, allowing a survey of a large number of
sources to be undertaken in a relatively short amount of total
observing time. *However*, the MOST *is restricted* to a single observing 2a
frequency, a relatively narrow continuum bandwidth of 3 MHz,
fixed right-circular polarization and a fixed physical configuration.

In the early 1980s, the pressing need for a frequency agile synthesis
radio telescope in the southern hemisphere was acknowledged. This
need was addressed by the official opening of the Australia Telescope
in 1988, with regularly scheduled observations commencing in
May 1990.

The Australia Telescope Compact Array (ATCA) is a   1d
sparse radio synthesis array, with 15 baselines compared to 351
for the Very Large Array (VLA) and 40 for the Westerbork
Synthesis Radio Telescope (WSRT). It was envisaged that to
provide good spatial frequency coverage, four separate observations
in different baseline configurations would be required to
adequately image a typical radio source. In practice, such usage
would have precluded the use of the ATCA to survey a large
number of sources. At the time, this raised questions such as:

Extending   • Was a survey of a large number of sources in a small number of
previous   observing sessions achievable?   2b
knowledge   • Would a "CUTS"-type observation with the ATCA be successful
                     for compact sources?
                  • Given the small number of baselines, could the resulting
                     images be deconvolved and used for quantitative analysis?

Occupying   This thesis presents the results of an observing programme which   3a
the niche   used preliminary Magellanic Cloud survey images from the MOST
                  to select sources to be studied with the then new ATCA. To test
                  the viability of the "CUTS" technique for the ATCA, a single   3e
                  12-hour observation at 4790 MHz was made in May 1990,
                  targeting seven sources and two calibrators in the Small Magellanic
                  Cloud (SMC) over I-hour cycles. The reduced data produced
                  images of satisfactory quality to enable quantitative analysis   3b
                  including the determination of peak and integrated flux densities
                  and the angular extent of the source. The observing programme
                  was therefore extended to include further sources in both Clouds
                  over a 12 month period. At that time only 5 ATCA antennas were
                  operational, giving just 10 baselines. The observing techniques
                  outlined here were extremely fruitful, and are now the basis for   3b
                  many continuum observations with the ATCA, made with the full
                  set of 6 antennas and 15 baselines.

                  The properties of 61 compact radio sources in the Clouds are
                  presented in this thesis, including flux densities at frequencies
                  from 408 MHz to 8.6 GHz, radio spectral indices, and the
                  presence of coincident X-ray emission and likely classification   3b
                  of the emitting object. These studies have had significant
                  scientific implications, including the selection of source
                  candidates for other survey work and detailed studies of individual
                  objects, two of which are the subjects of detailed chapters of   3c in
                  this thesis*.   part

* Move 3c, titled *Thesis Outline*, is found in full in 1.4 of this thesis chapter.

Source: Amy 2000: 1–2

Application

- Discuss the typical Introduction framework in terms of the three moves and introduce the notion of sub-moves. Wherever possible, illustrate the extent to which the framework can be used to analyse authentic thesis introductory chapters. Our students respond well to chapters that we download from sites such as the Australian digital thesis site http://adt.caul.edu.au/ and then discuss with them.

- Show students the extract from a thesis, explicitly entitled 'Overview', presented in Box 6.2, in which moves from the framework have been identified and labelled. It is important to bear in mind that not all sub-moves will necessarily be used and that moves (and sub-moves) may be recycled several times.

- Ask students to bring along theses from your field to analyse or provide examples of chapters for them to analyse and annotate themselves. Ask them to use the framework in Table 6.1 for their analysis. If some of the moves in Table 6.1 are not present, ask them to reflect on why they may not be there.

- Many students, not only non-native speakers of English, experience difficulty with verb tenses when reviewing the literature in a field. It may be useful to raise their awareness of typical tense usage through focusing on examples in your specific discipline. Similarly, an increased awareness of other language features can be of benefit to students. Alerting students to the range of ways in which 'gap statements' can be expressed provides second-language speakers of English with a useful resource. We have found that students find the concept of metadiscourse a particularly useful one. Exposing students to the range of verbs and nouns available to talk about one's research and the research process can extend students' linguistic resources. Ask students to examine the use of verb tenses in the Introduction to a thesis in your discipline. Ask them to explain why the tenses have been used the way they have (ask students to refer to the extracts on p.87 for suggestions for how to explain this).

- Ask students to use the framework in Table 6.1 to make a list in note or bullet point form showing what they will place in each section of their Introduction when they come to write it. Ask them to add to and revise this list as they work on their thesis, and then use these notes as a framework for writing their Introduction, when they get to this stage in their writing.

- In Box 6.3, a more extended extract is provided in which several of the moves are recycled and the organizational structure is more complex. Ask students to reflect on why this is. Ask students to identify moves from thesis introductions that you provide or which they have found.
- In Box 6.3, the initial paragraph is labelled as an 'advance organizer'. This term refers to sentences or sometimes paragraphs which preview what will be discussed later in the chapter. In theses they have an important role to play in helping the writer to organize the large amounts of information the thesis contains and they help the reader to relate the different parts of the thesis to each other. This type of organization is worth pointing out to students as it helps both writer and reader. Ask students to go through the introduction to a thesis in their area of study and identify whether the writers have used advance organizers. Relate this to the notion of 'reader-friendly theses' discussed in Chapter 3.
- Similarly, the use of sub-headings, often in combination with a numbering system, is becoming a common organizational feature of theses and, when combined with the advantages of the formatting features in word-processing packages, can provide a useful scaffolding tool for writers as their text develops (see also Chapter 9).

Box 6.3 Extract from Introduction of a PhD thesis in history

Chapter 1
Introduction and thesis
Overview

Introduction

Advance organizer

In this introductory chapter the background to the present research study will be provided along with an outline of the principal theoretical propositions. The chapter will also set out the research problem and the associated research questions that the thesis seeks to address. The justification for the research and a statement of the contribution the thesis makes to the field of sports studies follows. Finally, a brief overview of research methodology will be included along with an outline and diagrammatic representation of the structure of this thesis.

Occupying the niche

This thesis is an investigation of the sporting experiences of women   3a
from culturally and linguistically diverse backgrounds in Australia.
Women from diverse cultural and linguistic backgrounds are a sub-population that has been identified as the 'other' in previous research

Establishing a research territory	(hooks, 1989; Prakash, 1994). Sport theorists that have researched 'otherness' suggest that individuals and groups from outside the mainstream have been historically marginalised in dominant discourses of sports (Bhandari, 1991; Hargreaves, 1992; Long *et al.* 1997). In Australia, the under-representation of this subgroup of women has been quantitatively documented across all dimensions of sports involvement. Previous studies have indicated that women from culturally and linguistically diverse backgrounds are significantly less likely to participate in sports activities (Australian Bureau of Statistics, 1998), engage in physical activity (Armstrong, Bauman and Davies 2000) or become sports spectators (Australian Bureau of Statistics, 1998). Women from culturally and linguistically diverse backgrounds are also less likely to hold either volunteer roles or paid positions in sports organisations (Fitzpatrick
Establishing a niche	and Brimage, 1998). *However,* existing research does not explore on why this under-representation occurs. Neither does it comment on how females from culturally and linguistically diverse backgrounds
Occupying the niche	think about and experience sports. The research undertaken for this thesis seeks to explore how the construction of sports discourses and the organisation of sports have influenced these women's sports experiences. It will be argued that the formation of gender and ethnicity relations in sports organisations has been constituted by culturally institutionalised meanings, actions and explanations that are systemically exclusionary of women from diverse cultural
Establishing a niche	backgrounds. As such, this thesis responds to the call to action by many sports studies academics who have suggested that research about migrant women and sports has been neglected for far too long (Costa and Guthrie, 1994; Hall, 1996;
Occupying the niche	Hargreaves, 1994; Theberge and Birrell, 1994a). The research focuses on the intersecting domains of gender, sports and ethnicity and the implications thereof for sports theory and practice. It has been previously identified that existing research on this topic is sparse (Adair and Varnplew, 1997; Australian Sports Commission, 2000; Booth and Tatz, 2000; Hall, 1996;
Indicating the gap	Mosely, 1997; Rowe and Lawrence, 1996). Given the identified gap in sports studies, this thesis has the potential to provide a better theoretical and practical understanding of sports, gender and cultural diversity.
	Women's studies, sports studies and migration studies have each developed their own philosophical and conceptual approaches to researching their constituent populations but each has seemingly
Indicating gaps	neglected theory development about the nexus between women, sports and ethnicity. Over the last few decades feminist studies have extensively and intensively debated the role that cultural institutions

Right margin annotations:
1b & c
2a
3a
3d
2b
3a
2a
2a

play in promulgating male hegemony; the ensuing power relations that are created, maintained and reinforced by these institutions; and the opportunities that women have to contest and resist a gendered construction of society. Initial feminist treatises proposed grand theories, which were applied to all women, however these theoretical assumptions have now shifted and recent works recognise that 'women' are not a homogenous group. In particular, feminists have delved into issues surrounding the marginalisation of women who do not fit into Eurocentric, middle-class, Western 'White' theorisation within poststructural theory (Prakash, 1994; Spivak, 1988). Poststructural feminists have further suggested that all studies of women need to acknowledge non-white, ethnic minority women and rethink how social identities and forms of knowledge can encompass the 'other' (hooks, 1989).

Establishing a niche in feminist literature — 2b

Research on questions of racial and cultural differences in sports appears to have been slow to respond to poststructural feminist imperatives, with research primarily located within androcentric paradigms (Thommson, 1998).

Gap in sports studies — 2a

Source: Taylor 2000: 1–2

Conclusion

The CARS framework has been found to be a useful way of assisting thesis writers with developing a structure for their Introduction that enables them to clearly indicate to the reader what the significance of their thesis is. It should not however be seen as rigid and inflexible: it is a tool for understanding how writers within different disciplines attempt to persuade their readers of the validity of their arguments for the research space they have created.

Writers of completed theses will often report that the Introduction was the last chapter that they wrote and many experienced writers of journal articles report a similar phenomenon. For some, the introductory section is one of the hardest to write. While it can be argued that one only knows where one is going once one has arrived and that is why the Introduction can only be written at the end of the journey, it is important to at least draft the Introduction – and the research proposal will, to a degree, be that draft – so that it can be redrafted as the thesis evolves until finally the overall meaning of the thesis emerges. As Levine (2002) puts it, Chapter 1 – the Introduction – needs to be 'rewritten' with the insights gained from having drafted the complete thesis. The Introduction may also 'tidy up' the somewhat messy, circular process of the research and make it appear more linear and logical.

A final point concerns the article-compilation thesis – a collection of published papers, prefaced by an Introduction and a concluding chapter – which is becoming more common in the science, technology and engineering fields (as discussed in Chapter 5). Dong's (1998) findings suggest that this new format changes somewhat the relationship between student and intended audience as the readership now becomes the wider scientific community of peers and not just the supervisors and examiners. Whether this shift in the status of the student writer impacts on the way the writer positions him- or herself in the Introduction has not yet been explored but is an issue worth considering when assisting graduate students who are embarking on the article-compilation type thesis.

Chapter 7

Writing the background chapters

Introduction

This chapter covers writing the background chapters for a thesis or dissertation. This includes writing the literature review and chapters which describe the theoretical framework to a study. Particular writing skills covered include summarizing and critiquing previous research, adopting a stance and using reporting and evaluative verbs. Attention is given to the issue of plagiarism and suggestions are made for how students can avoid it.

Writing the literature review

There are a number of purposes for reviewing the literature when writing a thesis or dissertation. One important purpose of a literature review is to contextualize the student's research. This review may focus on previous research on the topic, or it may focus on background theory which is relevant to the project, or both.

The review should describe and synthesize the major studies related to the topic of the research. It should also demonstrate the relationship between the student's project and what else has been done in the particular area. An important feature of the literature review that many students are not aware of is the need for it to be an extensive review of previous research, right up to their date of examination. This is especially the case at the doctoral level where the review of the literature is expected to be at a 'state-of-the-art' level. That is, the student needs to show they are aware of research relevant to their project that has been published right up to the point of submitting their thesis for examination.

In their book *How to Get a PhD*, Phillips and Pugh (2005) list four areas that need to be focused on in a research thesis. These are *background theory*, *focal theory*, *data theory and contribution*, as summarized below.

- Background to the study: a state-of-the-art review of the field of study, including current developments, controversies and breakthroughs, previous research and relevant background theory;

- Focus of the study: what is being researched and why;
- Data used in the study: justification for the choice of data;
- Contribution of the study: importance of the project for the field of study.

The first of these, background theory, is covered in most detail in the literature review chapter/s. This backgrounding of the project should lead to what is being researched and why. That is, the background chapters should lead to the gap (or gaps) in the field that the thesis or dissertation is aiming to fill.

All of this will vary depending on the level of thesis or dissertation the student is working on. Table 7.1, taken from Hart's (1998) book *Doing a Literature Review,* summarizes these differences. As can be seen from this table, the higher the level of study, the more depth and breadth is expected in the review of the literature.

What needs to be included in a review of the literature

A literature review needs to focus on the major findings of the studies that are reported on, when they were carried out and who they were carried out by. Reports on studies directly related to the student's project should be discussed in more detail, including information about the methodological approach used, data collected and analytical procedures used on the study. The literature review also needs to include critical comment on these studies, telling the reader which are the best studies, and why, rather than just presenting factual information about the studies that are being reviewed.

Table 7.1 Degrees and the nature of the literature review

Degree and research product	Function and format of the literature review in research at these levels
BA, BSc, BEd project	Essentially descriptive, topic focused, mostly indicative of main current sources on the topic. Analysis is of the topic in terms of justification
MA, MSc, MPhil dissertation or thesis	Analytical and summative, covering methodological issues, research techniques and topics. Possibly two literature-based chapters, one on methodological issues, which demonstrates knowledge of the advantages and disadvantages, and another on theoretical issues relevant to the topic/problem.
PhD, DPhil, DLitt thesis	Analytical synthesis, covering all known literature on the problem, including that in other languages. High level of conceptual linking within and across theories. Critical evaluation of previous work on the problem. Depth and breadth of discussion on relevant philosophical traditions and ways in which they relate to the problem.

Source: Hart 1998: 15

This is something many second-language students find especially difficult. In short, the literature review should focus on:

- the key issues which underlie the research project;
- the major findings on the research topic, by whom and when;
- the main points of view and controversies that surround the issue being investigated;
- a critical evaluation of these views, indicating strengths and weaknesses of previous studies on the topic;
- general conclusions about the state of the art at the time of writing, including what research still needs to be done; that is, the gap that remains in the research that the study will aim to fill.

A literature review needs to be an extensive review of the area with reference to many sources and previous research. The literature review may be arranged:

- according to the various questions to be asked;
- according to the various topics and sub-topics that are central to the study;
- according to the specific variables in the study;
- chronologically from oldest to more recent research;
- according to different points of view;
- or a combination of these.

There is no single 'right way' in which to organize the review of the literature. Often the nature of the research problem will determine the organization of this part of the thesis.

Reviewing the literature: an example

Box 7.1 shows the section headings from the literature review sections of a PhD written on the topic of Chinese students writing in English (Cahill 1999). In this case, the student has two literature review chapters, one providing background information on the study, and the other outlining the theoretical framework he is using for his study. The first chapter looks at the context of student writing in Chinese universities. The second chapter looks at arguments that have been made about the influence of Chinese and Japanese ways of writing on students' English texts.

Box 7.1 Sample literature review chapters

Chapter 2: English majors in China: An ethnographic mosaic

A. Introduction: Ethnography in China
B. The college
    The campus and facilities
    The Chinese teacher
    The foreign teacher in China
    Strategies of resistance
    Traditional, modern, and independent students
    Silence
    Apathy
    The personnel file
    Conclusion
C. The production of English writing
    Phillipson and linguistic imperialism
    Attitudes toward English in China
    The curriculum and informal English study
    The traditional essay
    The writing classroom
    Conclusion

Chapter 3: The myth of the 'turn' in Asian text structure

A. Kaplan and contrastive rhetoric
    Kaplan's 'Cultural thought patterns' article
    Hinds' and Mohan and Lo's critiques of Kaplan
    Kaplan's 'Contrastive grammar' article
B. *Qi cheng zhuan he* in contrastive rhetoric
C. Hinds on *ki sho ten ketsu*
D. The *qi cheng zhuan he/ki sho ten ketsu/ki sung chon kyu* trope
E. *Qi cheng zhuan he* in Chinese scholarship
    Early historical accounts of *qi cheng zhuan he*
    The relationship of *qi cheng zhuan he* to the eight-legged essay
    The eight-legged essay in contrastive rhetoric
    Modern theories of *qi cheng zhuan he* in Chinese scholarship
F. *Ki sho ten ketsu* in Japanese scholarship
    Chinese origins
    Kubota's critique of contrastive rhetoric
    Japanese multi-part essay formats
    Multiple interpretations of *ten*
    A critique of Maynard's *Principles of Japanese Discourse*
G. Conclusion: Contrastive and non-contrastive rhetoric

Source: Cahill 1999: vii–viii

Application: arranging the literature review

Ask your student to make a list of topics they will need to cover in their literature review. Then ask them to arrange the list in one (or more) of the ways listed earlier in this chapter. Ask them to explain to you why they have arranged their literature review in this way.

Strategies for reading for a literature review

Cone and Foster (1993), in their book *Dissertations and Theses: From Start to Finish,* provide advice to students on steps and strategies for writing a literature review. These steps and strategies are summarized in Table 7.2 on p.104.

Application: gaps in the research literature

Ask your student to follow the advice given in Table 7.2 about reading for a literature review and then write a summary of gaps in the research literature on their topic. Ask them to use this summary to present you with an argument for carrying out their particular project which comes from their reading of the literature.

Providing background information

It is important in a literature review to provide enough background information to previous research so that the context of the proposed research is clear; that is, the literature review should describe previous relevant research, and the results of that research, in such a way as to indicate where the present proposal is 'situated'.

There are a number of questions that are useful to consider when describing previous research. Amongst these are:

- Who carried out the research?
- Who were the subjects of the research?
- Why was it carried out?
- Where was it carried out?
- How was it carried out?
- When was the research published?
- What was the result of the research?

Table 7.2 Steps and strategies for writing a literature review

Steps	Strategies
Locate relevant literature	Identify key authors and journals
	Use state-of-the-art articles
	Use computerized searches
	Use Google Scholar
	Scan tables of contents from key journals
	Use reference lists from articles, books and chapters
	Read primary sources
	Avoid the popular press
Critically read the literature	Identify themes in the literature
	Identify strengths and weaknesses of individual articles
	Identify strengths and weaknesses of the field as a whole
	Collect photocopies of articles
Prepare to write	Investigate expected length and format of the literature review
	Make a preliminary outline
	Organize the literature you will cover
	Limit the scope of the review to the topic at hand
Write the review	Write the introduction
	Write sub-sections
	Use transition markers and metatext (see Chapter 5)
	Synthesize and critically evaluate the literature
	Be careful not to plagiarize
	Practise summarizing and paraphrasing actives (see below)
Indicate the gap	Use the review to lead to your study and research question/s

Application: providing background information (i)

Ask your student to look at the following extract from a thesis that was written by a student on the language and learning needs of international students, and ask them to answer the following questions.

> Burke's (1986) survey of the experiences of overseas undergraduate students carried out at The University of New South Wales discovered that the most common difficulty identified by these students was an inability to speak out in classroom discussions.

- Who carried out the research?
- Who were the subjects of the research?
- Why was it carried out?
- Where was it carried out?
- How was it carried out?
- When was the research published?
- What was the result of the research?

Application: providing background information (ii)

Now ask your student to look at a thesis or dissertation in their own subject area and find an example of reference to previous research which answers all these 'background information questions'.

Reading, summarizing and critiquing previous studies

Seliger and Shohamy (1989) provide a useful discussion of points to consider in reading, summarizing and critiquing previous research. While not all of the points they make are applicable to all published research, they do provide a helpful starting point for students who are new to this kind of task. The section that follows is based on their advice.

When students are reading previous research on their topic, it is important for them to identify the research problem and to think about how the research relates to their own research. They also need to look for the argument in the report that explains why it was important to conduct the research. Published research is also a very useful place for students to look for summaries of other research on their topic. The task which follows focuses on each of these aspects of previous research.

Application: summarizing a previous study

Ask your student to read a key piece of research on their topic and answer the following questions:

- What are the major research questions or hypotheses in the study?
- What were the main findings of the study?
- Why was it important to carry out the research?
- What is the relationship between this study and the student's own project?
- What other research studies were conducted in the same area?
- What is the relationship between these studies and the student's own project?

Ask your student to bring their answers to you for discussion.

Previous studies are also very useful for students to read, to learn about research design, data collection and analysis procedures. The following tasks ask students to read a previous study on their topic and identify how it was designed, how the data were collected and how they were analysed.

Application: summarizing research methods

Ask your student to re-read the study they examined in the previous task and answer the following questions:

- What research design was used in the study?
- What were the main variables in the study?
- What data were collected for the study?
- Describe the population, sample, and selection procedures for the sample.
- Describe the data collection procedures used in the study.
- How were the data collection procedures developed?
- Were issues of reliability and validity considered?

Ask your student to bring their answers to you for discussion.

Application: analysis of the data

Ask your student to re-read their study and answer the following questions:

- How were the data analysed in the study?
- Were the analytic procedures quantitative, qualitative or both?
- Would you be able to re-analyse the data on the basis of the information provided about the analytic procedures?

Ask your student to bring their answers to you for discussion.

It is also important for students to be able to identify the key findings of a research study. They also need to be able to identity the relationship between these findings and other research on the topic. The next task asks students to read a study to identify its key findings as well as how these findings relate to previous research on the topic. This is something students need to do, especially when they write the Discussion section to their thesis (see Chapter 10).

Application: analysing findings

Ask your student to answer the following questions about their study:

- What were the main findings of the study?
- How do the findings relate to previous research on the topic?
- What conclusions does the researcher reach on the basis of their findings?
- What are the implications of the findings?
- What recommendations does the researcher make based on the findings?
- What recommendations does the researcher draw from the results of their study?

Ask your student to bring their answers to you for discussion.

Reporting on previous research

There are a number of ways a student can report on previous research. Three key ways in which this is often done are what are called *central*, *non-central* and *non-reporting* styles of reporting (Swales 1990, 2004). That is:

- an author is directly reported as being responsible for a particular finding or argument and placed in subject position in the sentence (central reporting);
- an author is reported as being responsible for a particular finding or argument but with their name being given less focus by being placed in brackets at the end of the relevant statement (non-central reporting);
- the results of a piece of research are presented with less focus being given to the author or the actual study and no 'reporting verbs' such as 'claim' or 'shown' are used (non-reporting).

Below are examples which demonstrate each of these styles:

- Central reporting: 'Burke (1986) discovered that many students would like to become integrated into Australian society.'
- Non-central reporting: 'It has been shown that students have often performed successfully in their own education system before they seek entry to the particular university (Ballard 1991).'
- Non-reporting: 'Instead of motivation producing achievement, it may be that achievement produces motivation (Spolsky 1989).'

Each of these reporting styles places different focus on the researcher. These are sometimes described as:

- strong author focus (central reporting);
- weak author focus (non-central reporting);
- no specific author focus (non-reporting).

Application: reporting on previous research

Ask your student to look at a literature review in their area of study and find examples of central, non-central and non-reporting styles. Ask them to think about why the author of the thesis chose to use each reporting style.

Reporting verbs

Many different verbs can be used to report on previous research. There are a number of ways in which these verbs can be classified. One suggestion is for their division into groups such as:

- verbs which make a *statement*, such as 'report';
- verbs which express, in a very general way, a writer's personal *judgment*, such as 'explain';
- verbs which express a writer's *opinion*, such as 'argue';
- verbs which present a writer's *suggestion*, such as 'propose';
- verbs which express some kind of *disagreement*, such as 'doubt'.

Application: reporting verbs

Ask your student to look at the list of reporting verbs and decide whether they are examples of statement, judgment, opinion, suggestion, or disagreement type verbs.

Some of these verbs are quite similar in how they may be classified. It is useful, however, to consider differences between them as not all of these verbs have the same meaning.

point out	argue	claim	state	doubt
propose	observe	identify	report	agree (with)
add	describe	say	explain	present
indicate	assert	believe	question	dispute
maintain	support	think	challenge	dismiss
recommend	say	urge	suggest	disagree (with)
claim	assert	affirm		

Students often ask what tense they should use in their literature review. Reporting verbs in a literature review are often in the *simple present*, the *simple past* or the *present perfect*. Table 7.3 shows examples of this.

Some suggestions for choices of tense and reasons for their use are shown in Table 7.4.

Application: choice of verb tense

Ask your student to look at the literature review in a thesis or dissertation in their own area and find an example of each of the above tenses being used in a reporting verb. Do they agree with the suggestion for the choice of tense made in Table 7.4?

Table 7.3 Typical tenses used in the literature review

Tense	Example
simple present	Brown (1989) *shows* that
simple past	Brown (1989) *showed* that
present perfect	Research *has shown* that

Table 7.4 Choices of tense and reasons for their use

Choice of tense	Reason
present simple	a generalization is being made a reference is being made to the state of current knowledge previous findings are being presented/are accepted as facts
simple past	a reference is being made to a single study a specific piece of research and its findings are being referred to
present perfect	a general area of investigation or inquiry is being referred to a general statement is made about previous research

Critiquing previous research

A key feature of a review of previous research is critiquing previous studies. This is something many second-language students find difficult to do. Below are some questions students may wish to consider in their reading and critiquing of previous work.

- Is the research problem clearly stated?
- Are the variables clearly described and defined?
- Is the design of the study appropriate for the particular research question?
- Are the research instruments appropriate for the particular study?
- Are the data analysis procedures appropriate for the particular study?
- Was the author consistent in the way they analysed their results?
- Are the conclusions, implications and recommendations warranted by the results?

Application: summarizing and critiquing previous research

Ask your student to read, summarize and critique a key study in their area using the set of questions outlined above.

Adopting a stance towards previous research

As students review and critique previous research, they also need to show their position, or stance, in relation to this research. They often do this through their use of evaluative language, or metadiscourse. This is a topic which Hyland (e.g. 2000, 2004a, 2005a, 2005b; Hyland and Tse 2004) has discussed in detail. Metadiscourse refers to 'the linguistic devices writers employ to shape their arguments to the needs and expectations of their target readers' (Hyland 2004a: 134); that is, their attitude and commitment to what they have read. Hyland lists a set of linguistic strategies that thesis and dissertation writers often use to comment on previous research and involve their reader in the argument they are making. These are summarized in Table 7.5.

Application

Ask your student to read a study in their area and find examples of hedges, boosters, attitude markers, engagement markers and self-mentions. Encourage them to make a list of these as they do their further reading.

Table 7.5 Linguistic strategies for commenting on previous research

Strategy	Function	Examples
Hedges	to withhold the writer's full commitment to a proposition	might/perhaps/ possible/about
Boosters	to emphasize force or the writer's certainty in a proposition	in fact/definitely/it is clear that
Attitude markers	to express the writer's attitude towards a proposition	unfortunately/ I agree/surprisingly
Engagement markers	to explicitly refer to or build a relationship with the reader	consider/note that/you can see that
Self-mentions	to make explicit reference to the researcher/s	I/we/my/our

Source: based on Hyland 2004a

Paraphrasing and summary writing

A further important strategy that second-language writers need to develop for summary writing is good paraphrasing skills. As Bailey (2003: 21) points out, effective paraphrasing is vital in academic writing for, among other things, avoiding the risk of plagiarism. A good paraphrase, in his words, 'is significantly different from the wording of the original, without altering the meaning at all'. Bailey suggests three key techniques students can use to do this. These are *changing the word*, *changing the word class*, and *changing the word order*. These techniques are summarized in Table 7.6.

Application: paraphrasing

Ask your student to take a small section of text from their reading and paraphrase it using the techniques of changing the word, changing the word class, and changing the word order.

Table 7.6 Techniques for paraphrasing and summary writing

Technique	Examples of the technique	Examples in a sentence
Changing the word	*Change* studies *to* research *Change* society *to* civilization *Change* mud *to* deposits	*Change* Sleep scientists have found that traditional remedies for insomnia, such as counting sheep, are ineffective *to* Sleep researchers have found that established cures for insomnia, for instance counting sheep, do not work.
Changing the word class	*Change* Egypt (noun) *to* Egyptian (adjective) *Change* Mountainous regions (adjective + noun) *to* in the mountains (noun)	*Change* A third group was given no special instructions about going to sleep *to* A third group was not specially instructed about going to sleep
Changing the word order	*Change* Ancient Egypt collapsed *to* the collapse of Egyptian society began	*Change* There are many practical applications to research into insomnia *to* Research into insomnia has many practical applications

Source: based on Bailey 2003

Avoiding plagiarism

A number of authors have discussed the issue of plagiarism in academic writing. Pennycook (1996), for example, argues that plagiarism, for second-language students especially, is not a simply black-and-white affair that can be prevented by threats, warnings and admonitions. In his view:

> All language learning is to some extent a process of borrowing others' words and we need to be flexible, not dogmatic, about where we draw boundaries between acceptable or unacceptable textual borrowings.
>
> (Pennycook 1996: 227)

Some have argued that plagiarism is a culture-specific western concept. Others, such as Liu (2005), have argued that plagiarism is just as unacceptable in countries such as China as it is in the west. China, for example, has recently set up a website called New Threads (www.xys.org) which discusses, among other things, the topic of academic misconduct. One of the topics discussed on this site is the issue of plagiarism. In Liu's view, one of the reasons second-language students may plagiarize is their lack of language proficiency and writing skills, not their lack of awareness of the unacceptability of this practice. As Canagarajah (2002: 155) puts it, all texts are, indeed, 'intertexts' and behind all knowledge 'lies not physical reality but other texts, followed by other texts' as well as others' (often contestable) views rather than 'impersonal and absolute truths' (Abasi *et al.* 2006: 114). Students, thus, need to learn how 'to borrow other people's texts and words' so they will be able to achieve their rhetorical and intellectual goals (Canagarajah 2002: 156) as well as make it clear the work they are presenting is their own, not someone else's. Good paraphrasing and summarizing strategies are a key way in which second-language writers can learn to do this (see Abasi *et al.* 2006 for further discussion of this).

Conclusion

Writing the background chapters is an important part of the thesis and dissertation writing process. It is where students 'show what they know' as well as what they 'think about what they have read'. Students are expected not just to know the literature on their topic but also to critically evaluate it. The notion of critical thinking is a culture-specific western idea, however, even though it is often presented in the literature as a universal norm (Pennycook 1996; Canagarajah 2002). This notion, further, is often in direct conflict with some second-language students' cultural backgrounds and past educational experiences. Angelova and Riazantseva (1999), for example, report on a Russian student who said that where she came from it was dangerous to criticize people in authority as this would be seen as an act of subversion, and should be avoided. Their Indonesian students made similar comments. Scott (1999) reports on a Korean student who describes the notion of critical thinking as an ongoing struggle. Others, such as Jones (2001) and Canagarajah (2002), argue that second-language students are as capable of critical thinking as native-speaker students and that the stereotype of some second-language learners, as being 'passive and unable to think critically is flawed' (Jones 2001: 175). We agree with this view. It is not a case of whether someone is capable of critically evaluating other people's work or not, but whether they know what they are expected to do, and how they should go about doing it.

Chapter 8

Writing the Methodology chapter

Introduction

This chapter discusses issues to consider in writing a Methodology chapter that are of particular relevance to the second-language speaker. Students are often not fully aware of the purposes of this section. Second-language students in particular may not understand the distinction between methodology and methods where it is relevant. This may lead not only to inadequate description of the approach and framework adopted but also to an absence of argument and justification for the chosen approach. Students need to understand that one of the key functions of this section is to enable other researchers to replicate the study and this may account for the lengthier Methodology components of research theses as opposed to the more terse research article (Swales 2004). We also consider typical problems reported by an experienced examiner of PhD theses, many of which relate to an underdeveloped understanding of the role and function of this section of the thesis, and suggest ways to overcome these.

The evolution of the thesis genre has also meant that the standard introduction–methods–results–discussion format for reporting on research, in which the Methods or Methodology chapter typically appeared after the Introduction and/or literature review and was clearly identifiable as such, is no longer mandatory, with writers having greater choice as to layout and formats, more specifically in regard to qualitative research (discussed in more detail below). In fact, qualitative research presents particular challenges for the second-language thesis writer, some of which are considered in this chapter, in particular the presentation of the role of the researcher.

Selecting examples of Methodology chapters that you consider successful in your field to discuss with your students will be immensely valuable to them. We provide extracts from completed PhD theses that focus on specific organizational and language features that you may wish to draw to your students' attention. It is important for students to realize that simply looking at research articles to provide guidance on how to compose a Methodology section may not be adequate, as methods sections in contemporary scientific research articles tend to be 'extremely compressed', whereas in theses they are likely to be 'more leisurely and explicit' (Swales 2004: 86).

The place of the Methodology section

The location of the Methodology section in the thesis may vary. In the traditional simple thesis (see Chapter 5) it is typically a separate chapter preceding the Results chapter; in the thesis by compilation, each discrete study may contain its own Methodology or Methods section, as in Box 8.1.

In topic-based theses (more typical in the social sciences or humanities), there may not be a separate chapter with the title 'Methodology' or the

---

Box 8.1 Extract from table of contents of a thesis by compilation, indicating location of Materials and Methods sections

Table of Contents

Source: Hoolihan 2005: ix

chapter may have a more metaphorical title or there may be no Methodology component at all. In the extract in Box 8.2, from a PhD thesis in linguistics, Chapter 3 is titled 'Theoretical framework and methodology', emphasizing explicitly the relationship between the Methodology and the theoretical component of the thesis. Box 8.3 contains the first page of the table of contents from a recent sociology thesis. There is no immediately obvious Methodology component and the slightly cryptic chapter titles are characteristic of the 'new humanities' (see Chapter 5). Chapter 3 is titled 'Sensing the other: The catch of the surrendering self' yet is where the author 'outline[s] my methodological stance and the methods through which I undertook fieldwork and analysed data' (Robinson 2002: 14) – in other words, the typical components of a Methodology chapter. The sub-headings such as 'conducting research' provide a clearer indication of the chapter's concerns.

Box 8.2 Extract from table of contents of a PhD thesis in linguistics

Table of Contents
List of Tables and Figures
Acknowledgements
Abstract

Chapter 1 Why history?
1.0 Introduction: research objectives
1.1 Background for research
1.2 Parameters of research study
1.3 Organisation of the discussion

Chapter 2 History as discourse: a review of the literature
2.0 Introduction
2.1 History as discourse
2.2 Temporal meaning in history: a review of the literature
2.3 Causal meaning in history: a review of the literature
2.4 Appraising the past – history as evaluation: a review of the literature

Chapter 3 Theoretical framework and methodology
3.0 Introduction
3.1 Selecting a theoretical framework
3.2 The research process

Chapter 4 The genres of school history
4.0 Introduction
4.1 Modelling text structure
4.2 The genres of school history – the preliminary investigation
4.3 The key genres of history: concluding comments

Source: Coffin 2000: i–ii

Box 8.3 Extract from table of contents of a PhD thesis in sociology

Table of Contents

Source: Robinson 2002: iv

Alternatively, the chapter heading may be 'Research Design' (see Box 8.4). At the beginning of this chapter, the writer outlines the rationale for his choice of research paradigm.

Box 8.4 Extract from Research Design chapter of a PhD thesis in history

Note title of
chapter

Chapter 3

RESEARCH DESIGN

Use of first
person – 'I'

Writer builds
argument. Note
progression of
italicized verbs
used from
'describe' to
'argue'
Justification of
choice of
research
methodologies

In this chapter, I *describe* the research strategy that I have used to study the impacts of the Mississippi civil rights movement. Building on the conceptualization of movement outcomes presented in Chapter 2, I *present a more detailed consideration* of the empirical dilemmas for research on outcomes. This initial methodological discussion applies generally to studies of movement outcomes. In addition, I *consider* the Mississippi movement as a case study, in terms of its strengths and limitations. The majority of the chapter focuses on the two components of the research design: the qualitative case studies and the quantitative dataset of Mississippi counties. The analysis that flows from these two distinct research strategies is complementary. In fact, I *argue* that both are essential because each answers different types of questions about the relationship of movements to outcomes.

Source: Andrews 1997: 64

Application

Ask your student to examine the contents pages of three recent theses in your field and to report on:

- the location of the Methodology chapter or section;
- the chapter or section titles and sub-headings.

Ask them to reflect on why the writer has opted for the chosen format.

Methodology vs Methods

Methodology refers to the theoretical paradigm or framework in which the student is working; to the stance he or she is taking as a researcher (e.g. choosing a quantitative or qualitative paradigm) and the argument that is built in the text to justify these assumptions, theoretical frameworks and/or approaches as well as the choice of research questions or hypotheses. The Methodology develops an explanation as to why the research method(s) under discussion have been chosen. The section will probably require a restatement of research aims/questions and involve explaining to the reader how the chosen research method(s) will help answer the research questions.

In the annotated extract in Box 8.4, taken from the beginning of the Research Design chapter, the writer starts with an overview of the chapter in which he outlines how the Research Design combines both quantitative and qualitative components. He makes it clear that the chapter contains a 'methodological discussion' which will examine 'empirical dilemmas' in the area under discussion in the thesis – dilemmas that emerge from the theoretical issues discussed in the previous chapter relating to 'conceptualization'. In other words, part of this chapter will consider theoretical issues at a fairly high level of abstraction (the Methodology) although, as the writer tells us, the bulk of the chapter will focus on the qualitative case studies and quantitative dataset (the Methods).

In Box 8.4, we have italicized the key verbs that announce what the chapter will cover. The verbs begin with a simple *describe* but quickly move to higher order activities such as *present a more detailed consideration*, and *consider* through to *argue*, emphasizing that in this chapter the writer is building a justification for his selection of research design and approach.

Methods refers to the actual research instruments and materials used. The chosen methodology informs the choice of methods and what counts as data. For example, interviews, participant observation and discourse analysis are methods commonly used in qualitative research, whereas in quantitative research the methods and materials used in a laboratory or other experimental setting will require detailed description. The writer needs to discuss why a particular method was selected and not others. The writer should refer to the literature on the method(s) under review and justify their choice using the literature. The justification should revolve around the intrinsic value of the research method chosen in terms of yielding the data that will enable the student to answer the research questions but could also address issues like limited time, the fact that it is a preliminary study, financial constraints, etc.

In Box 8.5 on p. 120, taken from the introduction to a Methodology chapter, the writer overviews her research questions and describes the methods used to collect the data as well as the rationale for the selection of what counted as data in the thesis. Her research methods include use of a questionnaire survey, interviews and a case study. We are also told that the chapter will explain the sampling procedures used, what the questionnaires and interviews consisted of, how the netball case study was developed and how the data was analysed. All the above constitute key components of a Methodology section, specifically the description and justification of the choice of research methods.

Box 8.5 Extract from Methodology chapter of a PhD thesis

Note title of
chapter

CHAPTER FIVE: METHODOLOGY

5.1 Introduction

Review

Preview of
this chapter

Restatement
of research
aims

Justification
of choice of
research
methods

Overview of
specific
methods
used

The thesis research questions were outlined in Chapter One along
with an overview of the methodology used to empirically investigate
the associated propositions. This chapter provides further details of
the methodology and fieldwork undertaken to collect data to analyse
the research questions.

The research problem is: to investigate how sports discourses,
organisations and practices have influenced the sporting experiences
of women from culturally and linguistically diverse backgrounds.
The primary data collected served two key functions. First, data were
used for the macro level purpose of revealing the 'big picture' about
women, sports and ethnicity. Macro level data and statistics on sports
and females from culturally and linguistically diverse backgrounds
were obtained via a questionnaire survey method. Second, micro level
information represents individual accounts of the situation.
Individual interviews were undertaken to complement and
personalise the data collected in the surveys and provide women with
the opportunity to tell their own stories. The data set was further
augmented by the use of an applied case study to explore application
and practice in netball. This chapter provides a detailed account of
the specific research methods employed, sampling procedures,
questionnaire and interview content and protocol, case study
methodology and data analysis techniques.

Source: Taylor 2000: 144

A review of methods used by similar studies

A sophisticated Methodology chapter will review the methods used by other
(seminal) studies in the student's area and comment on their limitations and
strengths in terms of the methods utilized. In Box 8.6, the writer provides
three major justifications for his choice of the unit of analysis. The final one is
the existence of a substantial body of literature which not only gives support
to the writer's choice of 'unit of analysis' but will also allow the writer to
locate himself within a tradition and enable his results to be compared to the
'broader body of research'. Thus we see clearly that the description of the
methods employed should never be merely a description but always link to
the writer's broader rhetorical purpose – to persuade the reader that this is a
serious piece of academic research, building on, while adding new knowledge
to, a solid tradition, by means of reputable methods of investigation.

Box 8.6 Example of justification of unit of analysis

Justification of choice of methods. Note use of organizational pattern – first, second, finally (our italics)	For the quantitative analysis and case studies I use counties as the unit of analysis. There are three major reasons for using counties rather than municipalities. *First*, the movement mobilized at the county level in Mississippi. There was often variation in the county in terms of which areas had greater levels of participation in the movement. Fortunately, the case studies allow me to examine this variation. Nevertheless, counties were a primary organizational unit because they were the most important political unit in Mississippi containing, for example, the County Board of Supervisors, the most significant political body in local Southern politics (see Black and Black 1987 and Krane and Shaffer (1992). This leads to a *second*
Reference to previous studies as further justification, including seminal study	reason for using counties as the unit of analysis – important outcomes can be measured at the county level. *Finally*, a large body of political research uses counties as the unit of analysis dating back (at least) to Matthews and Protho's classic study *Negroes and the New Southern Politics* (1966). Following in this tradition allows the results of this study to be compared to this broader body of research (see for example Alt 1994, 1995; Black and Black 1987; Colby 1986: Davis 1987: James 1988: Roscigno and Tomaskovic-Devey 1994: Salamon and Van
Anticipates results of study	Evera 1973: Stewart and Sheffield 1987: Timpone 1995 on electoral politics: Conlon and Kimenyi 1991 on schools: and Colby 1985 on poverty programs).

Source: Andrews 1997: 72–73

Applications

1 Discuss with your student the overall role and function of the Methodology section. Provide them with the visual 'map' in Figure 8.1. Suggest they use the map structure to generate a mind map of their own Methodology section and its key components.

2 Ask your students to examine Methodology sections from a couple of recent theses in their field in terms of the following questions:

- Was there a justification of the choice of methodology, theoretical framework or research design?
- Which elements of the 'visual map' were included?
- How were these elements ordered and was a justification offered for their choice?
- How 'reader-friendly' was the section?
- Did the writers discuss limitations to the research or problems they encountered during the research?

How the research was conducted and how the data were obtained

In addition, the Methodology section should explain how the research was conducted and how the data were obtained: how the particular method(s) were used. This section will require a detailed description of the research processes and procedures as well as an explanation of the reasons for doing so. Writers should consider the extent to which the method(s) chosen have shaped their data. For example, in qualitative research, writers will need to describe:

- how they obtained their informants or drew their sample;
- the location/setting of interviews;
- the themes covered in the interview;
- piloting, adjustments made, reasons for this;
- how they overcame obstacles they encountered.

Knowing how the data were collected helps the reader evaluate the validity and reliability of the results as well as the conclusions that are drawn from them. Replicability of the study is also an important consideration and is another reason for the detailed description of methods and procedures. In Box 8.7 on p.124, the writer clearly sets out the four sources of his data and then goes on to describe each in turn while highlighting the strengths and limitations of each of the sources.

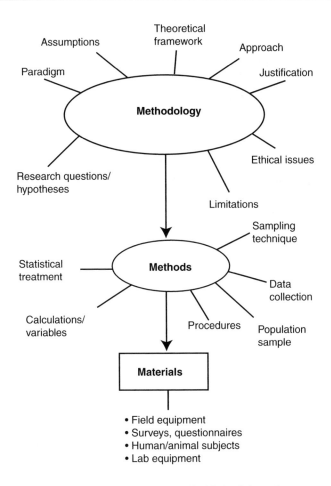

Figure 8.1 Visual map of typical components of a Methodology chapter

In a recent study of master's project reports in computer science, Harwood (2005) found that students included discussion not only of procedures used but also of procedures that could have been followed but were not, and of procedures that were attempted but failed. This feature of the thesis has also been noted by Swales and Feak (2000) and again distinguishes the thesis from the published journal article where the researcher may not mention the 'blind alleys and false starts ... integral to the research process' (Harwood 2005: 254). In the PhD thesis, in particular, the writer may be seeking to alert other researchers to potential pitfalls as well as to defend him- or herself from possible criticism that they had not considered all available options.

In Box 8.8 on pp. 125–126, from the section titled 'Materials and Methods' of a thesis in marine biology, the writer provides us with an extremely detailed

---

Box 8.7 Description and evaluation of data sources

	Data
Explanation of sources of research data	The research for this study was derived from four major sources: (1) archival collections of participants, civil rights organizations, and government agencies, (2) informant interviews, (3) newspapers, and (4) reports and documentation of various organizations
Reference to strengths and weakness of different methods.	and agencies such as the United States Commission on Civil Rights. Let me describe each in turn, highlighting the limitations and strengths of each.
	Archival Collections
	By far, the most valuable source of data for this study was the archival collections that document mobilization
Writer begins evaluation of source.	at the local level. The major collections consulted for this study are listed in Appendix B. Nevertheless, one limitation of the archival collections is the almost exclusive documentation of major civil rights organizations (e.g. CORE and SNCC) and the early 1960s: this limitation is reflected in the historical scholarship.

Source: Andrews 1997: 88–89

---

description of the research setting and of the methods and materials used in the fish tagging programme. The information provided would enable the study to be replicated or adapted in a different context, in other words to be of use to others in the field (Swales 2004).

How the data were processed

It is also essential to describe how the information obtained in the research process was analysed, prior to moving into a discussion of the results or findings. This section may vary in length depending on the amount of explanation that is needed in the specific field of study. The degree of explanation needed reflects the degree to which there is agreement or shared understanding in the field; the greater length of methods sections in the social as compared to the hard sciences suggests less unanimity as to methodological practice (Brett 1994). For example, statistical treatments such as 'Pareto curves' or 'multivariate analysis' may not need to be explained in detail as they form part of the shared and accepted procedures of a particular field (see Box 8.9 on p. 127 for an example of this). The language used is often impersonal, with verbs in the

Box 8.8 Extract from Materials and Methods section of a PhD thesis in marine biology

2.2 Materials and Methods

2.2.1 ERWDA cooperative tagging program

Location of study and background information

Detailed description of procedures and materials allowing for replication

Overall note: language used is impersonal. Researcher is not mentioned explicitly

A cooperative tagging program was developed through the Environmental Research and Wildlife Development Agency (ERWDA) in Abu Dhabi to administer the deployment of conventional tags on sailfish in the southern Gulf. Recreational fishermen and charter fishing captains volunteered to tag and release sailfish to advance scientific knowledge and promote conservation of the species. Captures were accomplished using standard sportfishing techniques including trolling with lures, as well as dead and live baits. Both circle and 'J' hooks were used, however circle hooks were nearly always used when live baiting. Tagging activities took place during private fishing excursions and fishing tournaments using FloyTM (Seattle, Washington) model FIM-96 small size billfish tags. Each tag consists of an 11 cm length of yellow colored polyolefin tubing with a unique serial number, return address and telephone number and notice of reward printed along the tag. A medical grade nylon dart is affixed to the tag with a short length of monofilament line. Data cards having corresponding serial numbers along with information fields for date of release, latitude, longitude, weight, lower jaw – fork length, angler and captain address details and remarks were distributed with each tag (Fig. 2–1). Tags were infixed approximately 4 cm into the epaxial muscle with a standard stainless steel applicator tipped tagging pole. Tagging was normally conducted while the sailfish were in the water, but in some instances when measurements were required the animal would be lifted onboard the vessel. Standard practice included removing the hook prior to release and using revival procedures (towing fish slowly behind the vessel), when necessary.

Billfish tagging report Tag No: E03406

Use of visual
reproduction
to illustrate
material used

(PLEASE FILL IN DETAILS AND RETURN IMMEDIATELY)

SPECIES	النوع	DATE (dd/mm/yy)	التاريخ
LATITUDE	المكان	WEIGHT Lbs. or Kg	الوزن
LONGITUDE	حد الطول	LENGTH in or cm	الطول
ANGLER	الصياد	CAPTAIN	القبطان
ADDRESS	العنوان	ADDRESS	العنوان
CITY/STATE/COUNTRY	المدينة / البلد	CITY/STATE/COUNTRY	المدينة / البلد
TEL./FAX	رقم الهاتف/رقم الفاكس	TEL/FAX	رقم الهاتف/رقم الفاكس
CONDITION OF FISH/REMARKS			البلا حظات

Figure 2.1 Billfish tagging data card (not to scale)

Source: Hoolihan 2005: 17–18

passive voice, in order to focus on the processes involved (see Box 8.10 on
p. 128). This section should also discuss any problems encountered with the
analysis or limitations.

Ethical issues

It is vitally important that the second-language student be explicitly made
aware of your university's ethical research requirements. International students in particular may need guidance in this regard. Issues of informed
consent, anonymity, the need for the informant to emerge unharmed from the
experience, and power relations are key considerations. Students may need
help with drafting questionnaires (see Chapter 2) or to be directed to support
services if carrying out interviews in English.

The particular challenges of qualitative research

There is evidence to suggest that the second-language student may avoid
doing and writing about qualitative research because of the perceived linguistic challenges involved. Belcher and Hirvela (2005: 188) note having
observed second-language students being repeatedly discouraged, both by
their peers and by their academic faculty, from 'taking the qualitative route'.
In a study of the issues faced by Hong Kong scholars writing for publication,
Flowerdew (1999: 257) reported the perception of several of his interviewees
that non-native speakers of English are better suited to writing in the more

Box 8.9 Account of how data were processed from a PhD thesis in marine biology

2.2.3 Modeling analyses

Detailed account of how data were processed. Note that Brownie *et al.* model class is not described in detail but simply referred to

The "Brownie *et al.* Recoveries" model class in program MARK (White and Burnham 1999) was used to estimate probabilities of sailfish survival (S) and tag-recovery rates (f) from the harvest of previously tagged fish. Survival rates are useful in that they often have the greatest impact on population growth rates; although in terrestrial species recruitment is the bigger force. The required input file for program MARK was constructed from individual encounter histories using a binary code of 1 or 0 to designate whether or not an animal was encountered on a particular occasion (Fig. 2–2).

Justification of type of analysis used

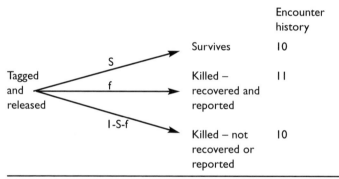

Figure 2–2. History coding for dead recoveries (redrawn from White and Burnham 1999).

Source: Hoolihan 2005: 20–21

Box 8.10 Use of impersonal language in data analysis section of a PhD thesis in marine biology

Description of how data processed. Note use of passive voice and impersonal style. Who analyzed the data is not considered important. Impersonal verbs in passive voice are italicized

Tagging data *were placed* on a SQL server and accessed through a proprietary software program that included forms for issuing, deployment and recapture of tags. In addition to basic search facilities, specific report writing functions were available to monitor levels of angler/captain participation and the temporal and spatial aspects of sailfish movements. The tagging data *were analyzed* to determine recapture rates, days at liberty, distance traveled (linear displacement), spatial pattern of recaptures and estimates of probability for survival and recovery. During the period of 19 November 1998 to 7 April 2004 a total of 2053 ERWDA tags *were deployed* on Gulf sailfish by 45 captains and 841 anglers participating in the program.

Source: Hoolihan 2005: 19

---

predictable formats typical of quantitative research articles in the sciences and engineering, in which the language used is 'quite simple and straightforward'. Qualitative research papers, as commonly found in arts and humanities, were seen as requiring more sophisticated language skills as well as lacking set formats. As noted by Miles and Huberman:

> The reporting of qualitative data may be one of the most fertile fields going: there are no fixed formats, and the ways data are being analysed and interpreted are getting more and more various. As qualitative data analysts, we have few shared canons of how our studies should be reported. Should we have normative agreement on this? Probably not now – or, some would say, ever.
>
> (Miles and Huberman 1994: 299)

Thesis writers who opt for the relative 'safety' of quantitative research will in all probability become writers of quantitative research papers, thus diminishing perhaps the likelihood of the unique cross-cultural perspective they might otherwise have brought to the world of international research (Flowerdew 1999). Those second-language researchers who choose the challenging formats of qualitative research may need to be particularly persuasive and articulate as they grapple with, for example, the complex theoretical frameworks, methodologies and innovative presentation formats of theses in very qualitative areas such as the new humanities. For, as Richardson (2000) has argued, in qualitative research, writing becomes an integral part of the research process. Nevertheless, more recently, Belcher and Hirvela (2005) have shown that with motivation, encouragement and support, second-language speakers may successfully rise to the challenge of writing a qualitative thesis. They point out, however, that the processes of qualitative research place 'particularly heavy demands on writers and language users' (Belcher and Hirvela 2005: 189), not only in the carrying out of fieldwork, interviews, observation, reflection and data analysis but also because the genres for reporting qualitative research are ill-defined and 'fuzzy'. So, as Turner (2003) advises, students should be made aware that there may be risks associated with challenging accepted forms of thesis writing and that successful theses should always be constructed around a convincing, intelligible argument whatever the methodologies or approaches involved.

Two of the second-language students interviewed by Belcher and Hirvela (2005: 199) had devised useful strategies for helping them to cope with the lack of a predictable format for qualitative research. Chantsvang set up a support group with friends who were writing qualitative dissertations: 'I found myself drowning in data ... I discussed what problems I had, and they discussed their problems as we tend to exchange our opinions'. Another student, Liang, found that reading a lot of qualitative research articles in her field helped her write up her data: 'I really read carefully how do TESOL scholars do their discourse analysis'.

Representation of the researcher (with special reference to qualitative research)

Academic writing is typically viewed as largely depersonalized. Textbooks tell students that for scientific writing to be objective, it should be impersonal and use the passive voice – thus removing or reducing the presence of the researcher in the text. However, in qualitative research the researcher's role is fundamentally reconsidered as he or she is no longer required to be an 'objective' and detached researcher. Writing accounts of qualitative research can prove challenging for student writers in this regard as they work out how to 'present' their role in the research in the written text. It is vital that thesis writers persuade their examiners that they understand the role of the qualitative researcher (Rudestam and Newton 2001). The extract in Box 8.12 clearly shows the writer's awareness of the need to make her methodological position explicit.

We find that one of the most frequently asked questions is whether the thesis writer can use the 'first person singular' (i.e. use 'I'). The quickest answer is usually 'it depends' which, while largely accurate, is, of course, not entirely satisfactory. The response we usually give students in our classes is that the conventions of the discipline and/or the approach chosen shape the choices available to the researcher as writer as to how they present themselves in the written text. This may be an area that the supervisor as an accomplished writer in a particular discipline may not be consciously aware of. We suggest an explicit discussion with the student on this issue as it is often of particular concern to the non-native English speaker. A quick examination of recent journal articles in your field will reveal the dominant pattern but bear in mind that in the PhD or master's the writer is still a student writing for an examiner, whereas in a journal article it is a case of a peer writing for a fellow researcher so this may have an effect on the choice of pronoun. Most importantly, encourage your student, when examining recently submitted theses, to look out for how the writer 'talks' about his or her role in the research – to what extent is the writer 'present' in the thesis? Ask them how the writer's choice makes them 'feel' – comfortable, uncomfortable and why?

In the extracts in Boxes 8.11 and 8.12, we identify some ways in which writers choose to make themselves present in their theses and talk about their role in the research process. Note that in Box 8.11, the writer, who has carried out participant observation research, refers to herself in the third person as 'the researcher', while in Box 8.12, after an extended consideration of the role of the researcher, under its own sub-heading, the writer engages in a reflection on her own background and its possible impact on the research. This elaborated discussion is a justification of the choice of qualitative research methods; of the validity of the data-gathering process and an explicit acknowledgement that research cannot be neutral and objective.

Box 8.11 Writer's representation of herself as researcher in a PhD thesis in linguistics

Researcher refers to herself in the third person as 'the researcher'.	The researcher worked as a TESOL in Geneva for two and a half years, spending one and a half years conducting the interviews with colleagues for the Geneva part of the study. Therefore, the researcher experienced first hand the life of a TESOL in Geneva.
She describes her role as participant observer in research process	The researcher gradually became accepted as a participant in the field, being involved in teaching and training during the first year. As a participant observer, therefore, the researcher listened to the problems of teachers and teacher trainers and administrators. The researcher was often privy to confidential information and reports. Whilst these were not used in the study, they helped to confirm or question some of the data.
	The researcher was invited to give guest talks, to train teachers in various institutions, and to become president of the professional development association of TESOLs in Geneva.

Source: Waites 1999: 62

5.2.2 Role of the Researcher

Explicit reflection on discussion of the role of the researcher, influenced by feminist methodologies

Feminists strongly argue that methodologies that disempower women in the research process should be contested. Some of the power-based considerations are the researcher's role, the social significance of the researcher's gender, the validity of research, which does not have emancipation of women as a starting point, and the use of creativity in the research method (Jarvie and McGuire, 1994:164). The latter two considerations have been discussed in the previous section; this section will address issues relating to the gender and role of the researcher.

'The researcher' referred to impersonally and generically as 'typical' qualitative researcher. Note use of substantial justification via the literature to persuade reader of the validity of the writer's choice of research design and research strategies

The relationship between the researcher and the research participants is critical in qualitative methodology, particularly in interview situations. One of the main strengths of this form of information gathering is its capacity to avoid the creation of a negative power relationship between the researcher and participant. However, inequalities of class, age, ethnicity, and sexual preference may all influence interview dynamics and thus the outcomes (see Cotterill, 1992; England, 1994) and therefore need careful consideration in the research design and implementation. Another aspect to negotiate is the researcher's capacity to accept and respect the interview participants' views, even if these are radically different or opposite to those held by the researcher. Even when the opinion of a study participant is disconcerting or discomforting for the researcher the researcher must respect the right of the interviewee to express such perspectives and must take such views into consideration (Cotterill, 1992).

[...]

| Transition from 'generic' researcher to the embodied, subjective writer of the thesis. Explicit reflection on the writer's own 'positioning' in the research. Explicit disavowal of positivist objectivity of researcher | As the researcher, where was I positioned within this research framework? As a white, English-speaking woman I should acknowledge that my interpretation and construction of knowledge of 'others' might be seen as coming from a position of power. My approach to this research has been shaped by my cultural background as a third generation Polish Canadian of working class origins living in Australia since 1982. Therefore this research is located within a perspective shaped by my cultural background, class, race and gender. Additionally, as a relatively active sports participant over an extended period of time I bring to this research my personal experiences of sports and a belief that sports participation can be a positive activity. |

Source: Taylor 2000: 150–151

Keeping a research diary (logbook)

While the logbook is standard in laboratory settings, the research diary is less so in more qualitative research domains. Supervisors should think of encouraging their second-language students to keep notes on a regular basis of what they did and why they did it, as well as any reflections on the research process. Not only will diary-keeping facilitate regular writing, but depending on the nature of the research itself, it may also constitute data for the thesis.

Application

The comments in the box below are drawn from a talk given in 1996 by Professor Mike King, Dean of Graduate Studies at Charles Sturt University, in which he listed criticisms typically made by examiners of Methodology chapters. Ask your students to:

- consider these points when reviewing other theses;
- review their own thesis in the light of these points when the final draft of the Methodology section has been written.

What examiners typically say about the Methodology (King 1996)

- inappropriateness of the methodology to the theoretical framework and perspective of the study;
- insufficient justification for the choice of methodology with respect to research questions;
- placing the methodological approaches within logic of overall design and so demonstrating appropriateness;
- failure to link methodology adequately to methodological literature;
- inappropriateness of methodology to generate the data needed to answer the research questions posed;
- failure to recognize limits and parameters of methodology used (generalizability and repeatability, etc.);
- appropriateness of methodology to sample;
- inadequate description of the methodological approach and framework;
- inadequate description of the instruments being used;
- inadequate description of the development and testing of new instruments or techniques;
- inappropriate, poor and inadequate statistical treatments.

Conclusion

Writing the Methods or Methodology section is often perceived as 'comparatively easy and straightforward' (Swales 2004: 224); as we have shown, underestimating the true role and function of the Methodology section and in fact the distinction between methodology and methods can lead to difficulties. In particular, the longer thesis as opposed to the shorter research article may require a more elaborated methodology component which may require multiple drafts as the student comes to understand the need to provide justification and argumentation and not simply a list of procedures followed and materials utilized.

Chapter 9

Writing the Results chapter

Introduction

This chapter describes the typical components of the Results chapter or Results sections of a thesis. It also identifies distinctions in the location of the results/findings within the thesis that may be attributable to the research paradigm used. The chapter also highlights issues that may present a challenge to the second-language writer and provides annotated extracts from two PhD theses that illustrate the organizational and linguistic features discussed.

Structuring the Results/Findings section

From this point on in the thesis structure, it is fair to say that there is greater variability than in the previous sections we have examined. The second-language student is confronted with options as to how to structure and organize their data, present the results or findings of their research, and begin to put forward the knowledge claims they wish to make. To a great extent, the discipline in which they are working and the research paradigm, whether quantitative or qualitative, will shape the decisions they make as to whether, for example, they opt for a separate chapter entitled 'Results' or 'Findings' or have a series of Discussion chapters which integrate findings and discussion of the findings, with no identifiable generic headings. In the thesis by compilation (see Chapter 5), each chapter will report on a discrete study and therefore discuss relevant results within the specific chapter, usually making use of distinct section headings. In qualitative research in particular, it is less likely that separate Results/Findings sections will be discernable. Descriptive chapter or section titles are common and, depending on the type of analysis used, organization is often thematic. The challenge that the second-language student faces is often organizational. It is important that students are aware of the possibilities available to them, and the supervisor can provide guidance in this area through directing students to take note of common practice in the field of study. Once again, it is worth noting that the published journal article may not provide an adequate model; its shorter word length does not allow for the extended presentation and discussion of results required in the thesis.

Purposes of the Results section

However organized in terms of chapters and sections, every thesis will contain presentation and discussion of results/findings. As Thompson (1993) found, prescriptive study guides may mislead students as they present Results sections as being purely 'objective' descriptions, without acknowledging that these sections inevitably contain argumentation and evaluation as well. It is vital that the second-language student understands that successful Results sections are never mere presentation or reporting but always involve selecting and ordering the data in a way that is designed to guide the reader to the understandings the researcher wishes the reader to come to. The writer must thus draw out the significance of the data, highlight significant trends and comparisons, and keep indicating to the reader where in the data he or she is being led. Linking figures and tables to text and selecting which data to highlight then becomes very important as the 'argument' is built up.

In the Results component of the thesis, writers typically use language for the rhetorical (persuasive) purposes outlined in Table 9.1. In Move 1, the information provided is both metatextual – referring to the overall structure of the thesis or chapter itself – and preparatory, in that it sets the scene for the

Table 9.1 Typical elements in reporting Results sections of theses

Move	Purpose
1 Presenting metatextual information	presents preparatory information by: previewing, linking, providing background information, referring back to methodology points to location of tables, figures and graphs
2 Presenting results	presents results (findings) presents procedures restates hypotheses or research questions states what the data are and highlights data for reader's attention provides evidence e.g. statistics, examples; frequently presents information visually (e.g. graphs, tables, figures, photographs)
3 Commenting on results	begins to interpret results and make claims looks for meaning and significance; may point to contribution to field makes comparison with previous studies (often for justification of method or procedure) may comment on strength, limitations or generalizability of results

Source: based on Brett 1994; Posteguillo 1999; Thompson 1993; Yang and Allison 2003 presentation of the results to follow. Sentences that point to the location of tables, figures and graphs also form part of Move 1 as they comment on other parts of the text. Move 2 contains the actual reporting of the results. Move 3 then begins to provide a commentary on or an interpretation of the results. These moves or stages tend to occur in the sequence 1–2–3 but may be recycled a number of times as the results are presented, in particular, the presentation of results move (Move 2) and the commenting on results move (Move 3). Move 2 is virtually always present in some form, while Moves 1 and 3 are less predictable. Note that Move 3 may sometimes be located in a separate 'discussion of results' section.

Move 1 – presenting metatextual information

It is advisable to alert second-language students to the need to utilize Move 1 as an organizing and signposting device to assist their reader (examiner) in locating the Results within the broader context of the research. In the extract in Box 9.1, the writer makes extensive use of Move 1 as she locates Chapter 6 within the overall context of the thesis, referring both backwards to her Methodology chapter and forwards to further Discussion chapters. The chapter has a thematic title with the term 'findings' appearing after the hyphen. The writer reminds the reader of her mixed method approach and her research questions (elements of Move 2) and this in turn necessitates a lengthy Move 1.

Box 9.1 Extract from Move 1 in Findings chapter of a PhD thesis in history

Thematic title + use of generic term 'findings'	**CHAPTER SIX: PERSPECTIVES FROM THE MARGINS – THE FINDINGS**
Metatextual move – indicates structure and refers back to previous chapter	**6.0 Introduction** Chapter Five identified the methodologies that were selected to empirically investigate the research propositions. This chapter reports on the outcomes of the data-gathering phase. The data collected and information are analysed in relation to the overarching research question posed in this thesis:
Research question restated	*What impact have the discourses and organisation of sports had on women from culturally and linguistically diverse backgrounds in Australia?*

Refers back to theoretical framework	Inherent in this question is the assumption that male experiences are different from female experiences and that women from culturally and linguistically diverse backgrounds have different experiences than those from Anglo-Australian backgrounds. The notion of 'difference' recognises that there is more than one valid form of representing human experience and through investigations of behaviours, activities, experiences, perspective, insights and priorities a better understanding of these differences can be achieved (Ross-Smith, 1999). This notion is explored in the subsidiary question:

What are the sports experiences and perceptions of women from culturally and linguistically diverse backgrounds; and are these perceptions and experiences different from those of other women?

| Refers back to methodology to introduce results: reminds reader of mixed quantitative

and qualitative methodology	Survey research and interviews were utilised to investigate these questions. The surveys were designed to address the subsidiary question, that is, to ascertain if females from diverse cultural and linguistic backgrounds had different sporting participation patterns from females of English-speaking backgrounds. The central question was qualitative in nature therefore interviews were used to address its concerns.

The empirical research component of this thesis encompassed four distinct phases that were detailed in the preceding methodology chapter. This chapter outlines the findings of the broad level investigations into women, ethnicity and sports.

Source: Taylor 2000: 173–174

Similarly, although more briefly, in the extract from a science thesis by compilation in Box 9.2 on p. 138, the writer begins the chapter with a preview of the chapter. The term 'results' is the chapter's first major sub-heading.

Move 2 – presenting results

This move is included in all Results/Findings chapters. In both Boxes 9.3 and 9.4 on pp. 139 and 140, the writer's use of the passive voice and the past tense in the descriptions of data-collecting procedures are italicized.

Box 9.2 Extract from a PhD thesis in engineering illustrating Move 1

	Chapter 5
Topic based chapter title	AQUITARD HYDROGEOLOGY
Metatextual move – previews chapter	In this chapter, the hydrogeological importance of aquitards *is considered* by examining geological controls on vertical leakage, such as permeability of the aquitard matrix and spatial heterogeneity within the aquitard-aquifer system.
	5.1 Results
Definition of terms used. Reader given outline of chapter organization	The various units *identified* in this chapter *are referred to* as upper, middle and lower silt units (based upon grain size analysis) and as numbered aquifer units. The specific location of these units within the Shepparton or Calivil Formations *is considered* after the detailed analysis data *are presented*.

Source: Timms 2001: 100

This usage is quite common and has the effect of focusing attention on the processes and procedures carried out. Both writers, from different disciplines, make use of tables to display data visually. These examples serve as evidence of the data collected and also allow the writer to highlight information for the reader's attention. Writers must refer to tables, figures and any other visuals in their text as shown in the annotated extracts in Boxes 9.3 and 9.4. It is essential to ensure that tables and figures are numbered sequentially throughout the thesis – e.g. Figure 3.1, Figure 3.2, etc., where the first number refers to the chapter and the second refers to the figure itself. Tables and figures must have legends that are self-explanatory and which define any abbreviations and symbols used in the table or figure. All columns in tables must have headings and units stated. All figures should be clearly labelled.

The language of Move 3 – hedging

In Move 3, the writer begins to interpret their results and make claims about their meaning and significance (see Table 9.1). The writer may also make comparisons with previous studies in order to justify methods or procedures followed and may comment on the strengths, limitations or generalizability

Box 9.3 Extract from a PhD thesis in history showing Move 2

<table>
<tr><td>

Note use of
heading and
numbering

Procedural
description of
survey design
and distribution
Verbs in passive
voice and past
tense italicized

</td><td>

6.2 Schoolgirl Questionnaire Survey

The following data relate to the questionnaire
survey that *was completed* by girls from schools
located in the three collection regions. The survey
was designed to collect data for the subsidiary question
and to provide the researcher with data on issues
and questions that *could be* further *explored* in the
interviews. Some 1150 questionnaires *were distributed*
and 972 *were returned* completed, the response rate
was 84.5 per cent. Respondent characteristics,
sports participation patterns and preferences *are
presented* in the following results sections.

6.2.1 Schoolgirl Respondent Demographics

</td></tr>
<tr><td>

Statement of
data. Certain
data highlighted
for reader's
attention

Tables are
referred to
in the text

</td><td>

Of the 972 questionnaire respondents 90.4 per cent
(880) were born in Australia and 9.6 per cent (92)
overseas. However, a sizeable proportion, 48.3 per
cent, had a mother born overseas and 63.7 per cent
had a father born overseas. The details on the girls'
countries of birth *are presented* in Table 6.1 and the
parental countries of birth *are outlined* below in
Table 6.2.

</td></tr>
</table>

Table 6.1 Non-Australian born distribution:
Schoolgirl survey

Country of birth	Number	Percent
Lebanon	12	14.2
Vietnam	6	6.3
China/Hong Kong/Asian	3	3.2
Italy	2	2.2
Greece	1	1.1
Other English-speaking country	30	32.3
Other NESB country	38	40.9
Total	92	100.0

Visual
presentation
of data in
table

Source: Taylor 2000: 176

Box 9.4 Extract from an engineering thesis showing use of Move 2

5.1.4 Physical description

[...]

Statement of results – use of passive voice (italicized) and past tense

Distinctive clay mineralogy *was observed* for each of the aquitards. The clay fraction of the deep aquitard *was comprised* of 66% kaolinite, and the middle and shallow units *were dominated* by kaolinite-illite and illite suites respectively. The highest proportion of smectite found was 38% at a depth of 52.7 m within the middle silt unit. However, the proportion of smectite clay increased towards the surface of the upper silt unit.

Data (evidence) presented visually in Table 5.2

In contrast to the upper and middle silt units, the indurated clayey sand *was dominated* by kaolinitic clay (Table 5.3), and contained traces of haematite, mordinite and siderite (Table 5.2).

Table 5.2 Bulk mineralogy of the indurated clayey sand at Tubbo (see Timms & Acworth 2002b, for mineralogy of clayey silt units)

Depth (m)	Qtz	Flds	Ant	Gyp	Clc	Pyr	Gth	Mgn	Hmt	Mord-enite	Side-rite
31	M	M	–	–	–	–	–	–	?T	?T	?T
31	M	M	–	–	–	?T	–	–	?T	–	–

D = dominant(>60%), A = abundant (60–40%), M = moderate (40–20%), S = small (20–5%), T = traces (<5%)
Qtz = qtz, Flds = feldspar, Ant = antase, Gyp = gypsum, Clc = calcite, Pyr = pyrite, Gth = goethite, Mgn = magnetite, Hmt = haematite

Total subsurface salt storage contained within clayey silt (35 m total thickness) was about 11.8 kgjm^2. Of this salt store, the upper silt unit accounted for 86%, or the equivalent to 102 tonnes/ha of salts within 15 m of the ground surface, if salt laden silt *was distributed* homogeneously over this distance.

5.1.5 Thin section analysis of indurated clayey sand

Highlights data for reader's attention

The nature of the indurated clayey sand (26–32 m), delineated in Figure 5.2, *was assessed* by thin sections prepared and *analysed* by the methods outlined in Chapter 4.1.4.

On a macroscopic scale, visual examination of thin sections revealed significant heterogeneity. Reddy-brown iron staining *was evident* parallel to bedding, along with other small-scale bedding and cross bedding features. There were also fractures evident that *were oriented* at an acute angle to bedding.

Source: Timms 2001: 106–108

of their results. The language the thesis writer uses to comment on the significance of their results will therefore be hedged in ways that are considered appropriate by the discipline (see also Chapters 7 and 10 for further examples of the role of hedging in academic writing). Hedging allows writers to 'suggest' explanations, make interpretations of their data and draw tentative conclusions. In essence, the writer seeks through the use of hedging devices to moderate their claims by anticipating and/or rebutting any potential challenges to their methodology and the interpretation of their data (see Figure 9.1 for examples of how writers typically hedge their claims).

Hyland (1996: 253) has pointed out that hedging is 'notoriously problematic' for second-language speakers as it involves drawing on a complex range of linguistic resources to persuade their readers of the validity and reliability of their research in ways that are at the same time precise, cautious and appropriately humble. In the examples in Boxes 9.5 and 9.6 on pp. 142 and 143, we draw attention to the writers' use of hedging in Move 3 to comment on their findings as they guide their readers to accept the interpretation of the results that they are proposing in a humanities and an engineering thesis. Words and expressions that allow the writer to hedge their claims are italicized in the two boxes. It should also be noted that the writers switch to the present tense for the commentary element of Move 3.

Numbering systems

It is becoming commonplace, if not accepted practice, to use headings, sub-headings and numbering systems in theses. Both of the theses annotated in this chapter make use of a numbered heading system to organize information. The second-language student in particular may be unaware of how useful adopting such a system can be in helping to organize large amounts of text. This is facilitated by word-processing software which enables the writer to set up a template with headings and sub-headings formatted in their chosen style from the outset. These headings can then easily generate a table of contents. Based on our experience, it would be wise for the supervisor to advise students not to use more than three levels of headings when writing. In other words, if using a numbering system as in Box 9.3, 6.2 is a sub-heading (level 2) and 6.2.1 a sub-sub-heading (level 3). Using a numbering system can also facilitate cross-referencing in the thesis; rather than referring back to exact page numbers, the student can simply refer back (or forward) to the section heading (e.g. 'as pointed out in 3.2.2'). We find that encouraging students to use headings and sub-headings is a valuable tool in helping them organize information in the text and develop the logic of their argument.

Box 9.5 Extract from Move 3 of Findings chapter of a history thesis

Comment move
Comparison to
previous research
(the 1996 Census).
Statement of data

In comparing the survey figures to 1996 census data on each local government area the sample can be seen to reflect community patterns of migration. In the 1996 Census data reports for Blacktown the proportion of Australian born persons was 67 per cent and those born overseas are mainly from the United Kingdom (5%), Philippines (3%), Malta (2%), the former Yugoslavian Republics (2%) and Italy (2%). These figures were mirrored in the school survey when the first and second generation respondents were combined; Australian born 60 per cent, United Kingdom (8%), Philippines (3%), Malta (3%), the former Yugoslavian Republics (2.5%) and Italy (9%).

[...]

Comment move
Justifies
methodology
and writer's
interpretation

Given the above comparisons *it is a reasonable assumption* that the schoolgirl survey was broadly representative of the community where each school was located.

6.2.2 Sports Participation and Experiences

Procedural
description

The schoolgirl participants were asked to respond to a series of questions about their current sporting involvement, attitudes to, and experiences of, sports. For the purposes of the survey data interpretation two categories of schoolgirls from non-English-speaking backgrounds were identified; the first grouped data set are girls born overseas in a non-English-speaking country (NESCI) n=92, the second are girls with at least one parent born overseas in a non-English-speaking country (NESC2) n=335 and the third category (ESC) n=545 represents all other girls.

Highlights data
for reader's
attention statement

Comparison with
previous research

Some 83 per cent of NESCI, 85 per cent of NESC2 and 85 per cent of ESC girls answered that they had participated in sports during the two weeks previous to the study. This data *implies* a much higher rate of sports participation than has been found in previous research, which has suggested that an estimated 40 per cent of girls are actively participating in sports by the time they reach 15 years of age (Fitzpatrick and Brimage, 1998). The high participation rate in this research *is more than likely* linked to the fact that the majority of respondents completed the questionnaire when in a physical education class and therefore had just participated in a sporting activity. The responses *should be viewed* within this context. Therefore no conclusions are drawn from these rates of sporting participation in the school environment.

Comment move.
Interprets results
Uses hedging to
moderate claims
made

Final sentence not
hedged

Source: Taylor 2000: 177–178

Box 9.6 Move 3 showing hedging in an engineering thesis

5.1.6 Falling head permeameter testing of core samples

Writer's claim is hedged	[...] Swelling of 0.5cm for instance, would be expected to increase the porosity from 0.42 to 0.52, an increase of 20%. Given the log-normal relationship between hydraulic conductivity and porosity, *it is probable that* such a change in porosity would increase permeability by about an order of magnitude (Neuzil 1994).
	It should also be noted that swelling may also have occurred prior to testing due to lower effective stress as the cores were extracted from the ground and during subsequent storage at atmospheric pressure. Without detailed laboratory and field measurements of core parameters it is not possible to quantify this artifact.
Hedging used to discuss writer's interpretation of results	Chemical reaction between the clay and the permeant *may also cause* varied *Kv* during tests, and between repeated tests. For example, flushing with sodic water *may cause* dispersion of the clay and decreased permeability. *This appears to be the case* for the clayey sand which *generally showed* decreased *Kv* both during and between repeated tests. This *may be attributed* to cation exchange of sodium which changes soil structure. Hydraulic conductivity of soils is known to decrease with increasing BAR of leaching water (Appelo & Postma 1996).
Support for claim based on prior research	

Source: Timms 2001: 109–110

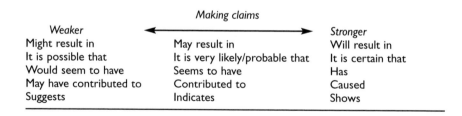

Figure 9.1 making claims: some examples of heding

Application

Ask your student to read two or three results sections of recent theses from either your school or department or an online repository. Ask them to identify an organizational pattern they prefer and to tell you which features of the organization they might use in their own thesis or dissertation.

Ask them to note:

- how the research results are presented;
- whether the three moves as shown in Table 9.1 occur;
- in what order they occur;
- the extent of recycling of the moves;
- the purpose of each of the moves;
- whether writers make claims about their results as well as describe them.

Conclusion

This chapter has focused on both the typical organizational patterns of Results/Findings chapters or sections and some of the language features commonly found within the different stages of the chapter. It is argued that for second-language speakers the need to understand the rhetorical purposes of this section is important and that to see the main purpose as simply being about the presentation of results may create a misleading impression.

Chapter 10

Writing Discussions and Conclusions

Introduction

The first part of this chapter looks at how Discussion chapters are typically organized and provides a framework that will help students write this section of the thesis or dissertation. Basturkman and Bitchener (2005; Bitchener and Basturkman 2006) have discussed the difficulties second-language students have with this part of their thesis. Students often lack an understanding, they argue, of the function of this part of their thesis or dissertation. As one of the supervisors they spoke to said: they thought there was a tendency for students to give more weight again to their own interpretations rather than use other academic texts to make or to support their claims (Bitchener and Basturkman 2006).

That is, students are often not aware of the need, in the Discussion section, to show the relationship between the results of their study and the results of similar studies and related arguments in the published literature. Bitchener and Basturkman also found that students tend to overstate their claims, partly perhaps because of their inability to 'hedge' in their writing (see making claims and hedging below). A further problem they noted is the tendency of students to mix the Results and Discussion sections of their thesis. Each of the students they spoke to in their study expressed uncertainty about what content should be included in the Discussion section and how it should be organized.

Functions of Discussion chapters

Rudestam and Newton (2001) and Evans and Gruba (2002) provide helpful advice on writing Discussion chapters. The Discussion chapter, Rudestam and Newton point out, is where the student should move beyond their data and integrate the results of their study with existing theory and research. A good Discussion chapter, they advise, typically contains the following:

1   An overview of the significant findings of the study
2   A consideration of the findings in the light of existing research studies

3   Implications of the study for current theory (except in purely applied studies)

4   A careful examination of findings that fail to support or only partly support the hypotheses outlined in the study

5   Limitations of the study that may affect the validity or the generalisability of the results

6   Recommendations for further research

7   Implications of the study for professional practice or applied settings (optional)

(Rudestam and Newton 2001: 121)

Strategies for writing the Discussion section

Evans and Gruba (2002) suggest strategies for writing the Discussion section. The first thing they suggest students do is to write down all the things they know now that they didn't know when they started the research, a single sentence for each item. The next step is to sort these sentences into some sort of grouping. Now the student should give headings to each of these groups of sentences. These will form the basis for the section headings of the Discussion chapter. Finally the sentences in each group should be given headings which will form the basis for sub-headings for each of the sections of the chapter. All of this can then be used to provide a tentative framework for the writing of this chapter.

Application

Ask your student to follow the steps outlined above for writing a framework for their Discussion chapter. That is:

- Write a sentence about all the things they know now that they didn't know when they started their research.
- Sort the sentences into groups.
- Write headings for each of the groups of sentences.
- Write sub-headings for each sentence in each group.
- Use this as a framework for planning the Discussion chapter.

The typical shape of the Discussion section

Research in the area of academic writing has shown that there are a number of ways in which Discussion sections are typically written. The Discussion chapter is often in a kind of 'reverse' form from the Introduction section. That is, in the Introduction the prime focus is on previous research on the topic, with the student's research, at this stage, taking a secondary focus. In the Discussion chapter, the student's study is the primary focus and previous research the secondary focus. Here, previous research is used for confirmation, comparison or contradistinction (Swales 2004).

Hopkins and Dudley-Evans (1988) looked at the structure of the Discussion chapters in master's theses in the UK. They found a number of steps that often occur in Discussion sections, as shown below.

1   background information;
2   statement of results;
3   (un)expected outcome – i.e. whether the result is expected or not;
4   reference to previous research – comparison of results with previous research reported in the literature;
5   explanation of unexpected outcome – i.e. suggesting reasons for an unexpected result (if this is the case) or one different from those found in previous studies;
6   exemplification – providing examples to support the explanation given in step 5;
7   deduction or claim – making a more general claim arising from the results of the study, e.g. drawing a conclusion, stating an hypothesis;
8   support from previous research – quoting previous research to support the claim/s being made;
9   recommendation – making suggestions for future research;
10 justification for future research – arguing why the future research is recommended.

Samraj (2005) carried out a study in the United States where she looked at the Discussion chapters of master's theses in the area of linguistics and biology. She found the Discussion chapters she examined typically followed the steps outlined below.

1   background information;
2   report on results;
3   commentary on results
        interpretation of results
        comparison with other research
        explanation for results
        evaluation of results
4   summary of results;
5   evaluation of the study;
        limitations
        significance/advantage of the study
        evaluation of the methods

6   evaluation of the field;
7   deductions from the results;
        research deductions
        applied deductions.

Another option for organizing a Discussion chapter is Swales and Feak's (1994) list of 'points' (rather than 'facts') that are typically found in the Discussion section of theses and dissertations. These are outlined below.

Move 1   Points to consolidate the research space – i.e. interpretive points rather than descriptive facts or results.
      For example:

- a reminder of the original purpose of the study;
- statement of results followed by a follow-up such as:
    - statement of the importance (or otherwise) of the results
    - examples from the data which illustrate the results
    - comparison with other work/previous research
    - review of the methodology
    - reference to the theory underpinning the study
    - conclusions that might be drawn
    - the strengths of the study
    - whether the results were expected or unexpected.

Move 2   Points to indicate the limitations of the study; what cannot be concluded from the research;
Move 3   Points to identify useful areas of further research.

It is important to point out, as well, that their 'list of points' does not represent a fixed order. Which point comes first and which comes next depends on the particular study. Also, Discussion sections often move through a sequence of steps more than once. Discussion sections, further, vary from discipline to discipline so it is important for students to examine what actually happens in their own field of study.

Application

Ask your student to look at the Discussion chapter in a thesis or dissertation in their area of study and make a list of the steps that it goes through. Which of the three models described above is it closest to? Or is it a mix of each of these?

Making claims and hedging in the Discussion section

Just as students need to show their position in relation to previous knowledge when they review and critique previous research (see Chapter 8), they also need to show their position in relation to the outcomes of their own research. That is, they need to show both their *stance* and *engagement* (Hyland 2005b) with their findings and the work of other researchers on their topic.

Hyland describes stance as the ways in which writers present themselves and convey their judgments, opinions and commitments to their own, and other people's, research. A writer may either: 'intrude to stamp their personal authority onto their arguments, or step back and disguise their involvement' (Hyland 2005b: 176).

Engagement is the strategies writers use to acknowledge and recognize the presence of their readers: 'pulling them along with their argument, focusing their attention, acknowledging their uncertainties, including them as discourse participants and guiding them to interpretations' (Hyland 2005b: 176).

The key ways in which academic writers do this and examples of each of these are shown in Table 10.1.

Table 10.1 Stance and engagement strategies

Strategy	Examples
Stance	
Hedges	Our results suggest that rapid freeze and thaw rates during artificial experiments in the laboratory may cause artificial formation of embolism.
Boosters	With a few interesting exceptions, we *obviously* do not see a static image as moving.
	This seems *highly* dubious.
Attitude markers	The first clue of this emerged when we noticed a *quite extraordinary* result.
Self-mentions	This experience contains ideas derived from reading *I* have done.
Engagement	
Reader pronouns	Although *we* lack knowledge about a definitive biological function for ...
Personal asides	And – *as I believe many TESOL professionals will readily acknowledge* – critical thinking has now begun to make its mark.
Appeals to shared knowledge	Of course, *we know* that the indigenous communities of today have been reorganized by the Catholic Church.
Directives	*It is important to note* that these results do indeed warrant the view that ...
Questions	*Is it, in fact, necessary to choose between nature and nuture?*

Source: based on Hyland 2005b

Application: stance and engagement

Ask your student to look at the Discussion section of a thesis or dissertation written in their area of study and find examples of the kind of stance and engagement strategies described by Hyland; that is, examples of hedges, boosters, attitude markers and self-mentions that express stance and examples of reader pronouns, personal asides, appeals to shared knowledge, directives and questions that express engagement.

Ask them to identify which of these strategies seem to be more common in their area of study.

Application: making claims

Ask your student to look at the following extract from the Discussion section of a master's thesis and look at the way the writers have made claims. To what extent, and how, have they hedged their claims?

> This would seem to suggest that knowledge of another European language did not prevent first language features from being carried over into English. If students did not transfer punctuation and stylistic features from French into English, there seems to be no grounds for assuming that they transferred discourse patterns from French. There appears to be a strong probability that the students' use of English discourse patterns reflects the fact that Arabic discourse patterns do not differ radically from English ones, at least in so far as expository texts are concerned. Written discourse may differ in the style of presentation between the two cultures, but the style merely reflects superficial syntactic differences, not contrasting methods of overall discourse structure.
>
> (Cooley and Lewkowicz 2003: 84)

Writing Conclusions

This part of the chapter provides a framework for the typical structure of concluding chapters. The language typical of concluding chapters is discussed in this section, as is the purpose of the Conclusions section.

Features of Conclusions

The Conclusions section is where students both summarize and 'wrap up' their work. Evans and Gruba (2002) list the following features of Conclusions:

- The Conclusions are what the Discussion chapter has been arguing for.
- The Conclusions may be a separate chapter or they may be combined with the Discussion chapter, labelled 'Discussion and Conclusions'.
- The Conclusions reached in this chapter should be drawn from the Discussion chapter.
- There should be no further discussion in the Conclusions chapter.
- The Conclusions should respond to the aims that were stated in the first chapter.

A summary of findings, they point out, is not the same as conclusions. Summaries are a statement of what the student found out; conclusions are a statement of the significance of what they found out. Often a Conclusions chapter is only a few pages long, as opposed to the Discussion chapter which should be much longer and much more extensive in its elaboration and reference to prior research.

The typical shape of Conclusions

Thompson (2005: 317–318) lists the following conventional sections of a Conclusions chapter:

- introductory restatement of aims, research questions;
- consolidation of present research (e.g. findings, limitations);
- practical applications/implications;
- recommendations for further research.

In his words:

> A thesis is a long text and the restatement of the aims and questions is a necessary reminder to the reader, several chapters on, of what the starting point of the research was. The concluding chapter is also an evaluation of the whole research project. This evaluation is strategically important as ... the targeted readers are also evaluating the project, to determine whether the writer is worthy of [the award of the degree]. In the conclusions chapter, therefore, the task of the writer is to point out what his/her achievements have been, and to forestall criticisms by identifying limitations of the research.

Bunton (2005) carried out an examination of the structure of Conclusions chapters in PhD theses and found two main types of Conclusions. He describes these as *thesis-oriented* and *field-oriented* Conclusions. A thesis-oriented Conclusion is one that 'focuses mainly on the thesis itself, beginning with a restatement of purpose and summary of findings and claims' (Bunton 2005: 214–215) whereas a field-oriented Conclusion 'focuses mainly on the field and only mentions the thesis and its findings or contributions in the context of the whole field' (Bunton 2005: 215).

He found these different orientations affected the organization of this chapter. Table 10.2 summarizes the typical structure and content of thesis-oriented Conclusions.

Field-oriented Conclusions, Bunton found, often have quite a different structure to thesis-oriented Conclusions. They are often written in more of a 'problem/solution/evaluation' type pattern and in some cases are written in the form of an argument. While this type of Conclusion is less frequent than thesis-oriented Conclusions, they do indicate that there is more than one way in which the Conclusions may be written. Conclusions also vary, Bunton found, across areas of study. For example, Conclusions written in the humanities and social sciences tend to be longer and have more sections than science and technology Conclusions. Students need to look at previous theses and dissertations in their area of study to see which of these patterns is more typical.

Application: the structure of Conclusions

Ask your student to look at the Conclusions section of a thesis and dissertation written in their area of study and to identify the organizational structure of this part of the text. Ask them to make a list of typical content that is covered in each of the sections that they identify.

The language of Conclusions

Hewings (1993) discusses typical language features of Conclusions. In particular, he describes how writers report, comment and speculate on their findings. He found, in his research, that writers typically refer to one of three things when they do this: the world, other research, and either the methodology or findings of the thesis or dissertation itself. Table 10.3 gives examples of this.

Table 10.2 The typical structure of thesis-oriented Conclusions

Section	Content
Introductory statement	Restatement of the issue being researched, work carried out, purpose of the study, research questions or hypotheses
Consolidation of the research space	Summary and evaluation of methods, summary of results/findings and claims
Recommendations and implications	Future research, practical applications, limitations of the study

Source: based on Bunton 2005

Table 10.3 Reporting, commenting and suggesting in the Conclusions section

	The world	*Previous research*	*Procedures used in the study*	*Findings of the study*
Reporting	The Malaysian government has set up a number of institutions.	Recent studies suggest that the greatest scope for increasing country exports of the products under study may lie in trade between developing countries.	The congestion costs were then measured for Britain...	Hire purchase was found to be the most popular and important method of financing fixed assets.
Commenting	Previous rounds of trade liberal-ization and the GSP scheme left the tariff escalation pattern virtually intact.	There are no examples in the data, but they might exist as, for example, evaluative comments on other work.	The scarcity of published research which is based on empirical bases about British marketing in PRC has forced the author to use a lot of publications from Hong Kong and America.	The information collected from the survey seems to suggest that small concerns rely more on ...
Suggesting	... there is a great need for an export insurance credit system to be implemented in Turkey.	Further research in this field would be of great help in the future planning of British strategies.	There are no examples in the data. Suggestions might, however, be made on, for example, the procedures that *should* have been followed in hindsight, given the results obtained.	There are no examples in the data. It is not in fact clear how this category would be distinct from Suggest-Literature.

Source: based on Hewings 1993

Application: reporting, commenting and suggesting

Ask your student to look at the Conclusions section of a thesis and dissertation written in their area of study and find examples of reporting, commenting and suggesting. How similar or different are they to the examples shown in Table 10.3?

Conclusion

The Discussion and Conclusions sections of a thesis or dissertation are, as Swales and Feak (1994) point out, not always easy to provide students with guidelines for. There is a lot of disciplinary variation in these sections. It is, thus, especially important for students to look at examples of previous theses and dissertations to see what writers typically do in their area of study. One thing writers do, however, in this part of the text, no matter what the conventions, is step back and take a broad look at their findings, and their study as a whole (Weissberg and Buker 1990), saying not just what the study has done, but also 'what does it mean'. This 'what does it mean?', we feel, is the key point that a good Discussion, and in turn Conclusions, section needs to address. A good thesis or dissertation should tell the reader not just 'what I have done', but 'why what I have done matters'.

Chapter 11

Writing the Abstract and Acknowledgements

Introduction

One of the final things a student needs to do is write their Abstract and Acknowledgements. The Abstract is an important piece of work as it is one of the first things an examiner will look at. The Acknowledgements are also an important part of the student's text as they can reveal a lot about disciplinary membership and networks at the same time as showing gratitude to the people that have helped the student in the pursuit of their studies. This chapter provides suggestions for how to structure thesis and dissertation Abstracts and Acknowledgements. Examples of Abstracts and Acknowledgements are included for students to analyse.

The importance of the Abstract

Cooley and Lewkowicz (2003:112) give this advice on the Abstract:

> [The Abstract] is written after the research has been completed and the writer knows exactly what is contained in the body of the text. It is a summary of the text and it informs readers of what can be found in the dissertation and in what order, functioning as an overall signpost for the reader. Although it is the last part of a dissertation to be written, it is generally one of the first a reader will look at. Indeed, if the Abstract is not well written, it may be the only part of the dissertation a reader will look at!

Typical structure of the Abstract

The Abstract typically aims to provide an overview of the study which answers the following questions:

- What was the general purpose of the study?
- What was the particular aim of the study?
- Why was the study carried out?

- How was the study carried out?
- What did the study reveal?

The typical structure of an Abstract, then, is:

- overview of the study;
- aim of the study;
- reason for the study
- methodology used in the study;
- findings of the study.

It is not always the case, however, that these will come in this order, as can be seen in the Abstract shown in Box 11.1. It may also be the case that they are not as neatly separated as they are in this text. These are, however, areas that are typically covered in a thesis or dissertation Abstract.

Box 11.1 Analysis of a PhD thesis abstract

Newspaper commentaries on terrorism:
A contrastive genre study
Abstract

Overview of the study	This thesis is a contrastive genre study which explores newspaper commentaries on terrorism in Chinese and Australian newspapers. The study examines the textual patterning of the Australian and Chinese commentaries, interpersonal and intertextual features of the texts as well as considers possible contextual factors which contribute to the formation of the newspaper commentaries in the two different languages and cultures.
Methodology used in the study	For its framework for analysis, the study draws on systemic functional linguistics, English for specific purposes and new rhetoric genre studies, critical discourse analysis, and discussions of the role of the mass media in the two different cultures.
Findings of the study	The study reveals that Chinese writers often use explanatory rather than argumentative expositions in their newspaper commentaries. They seem to distance themselves from outside sources and seldom indicate endorsement to these sources. Australian writers, on the other hand, predominantly use argumentative expositions to argue their points of view.

	They integrate and manipulate outside sources in various ways to establish and provide support for the views they express. These textual and intertextual practices are closely related to contextual factors, especially the roles of the media and opinion discourse in contemporary China and Australia.
Aim of the study	The study, thus, aims to provide both a textual and contextual view of the genre under investigation in these two languages and cultures.
Reason for the study	In doing so, it aims to establish a framework for contrastive rhetoric research which moves beyond the text into the context of production and interpretation of the text as a way of exploring reasons forlinguistic and rhetorical choices made in the two sets of texts.

Source: based on Wang 2006

Application: analysing an Abstract

Ask your student to look at the following Abstracts and identify these stages:

- overview of the study;
- aim of the study;
- reason for the study;
- methodology used in the study;
- findings of the study.

The political and educational implications of gender, class and race in Hollywood film: holding out for a female hero

This thesis examines the articulations of gender, class, and race in a specific sample of films from the 1930s to the 1990s. The tendency in these films is to depict women as passive, rather than heroic. Because this has been the common practice, I chose to outline it through fourteen films that exemplified an inherent bias when dealing with women as subject matter. Brief summaries of several recently produced progressive films are provided to show that it is possible to improve the image of women in film, hence we may finally witness justice on the big screen.

In this discursive analysis, I trace specific themes from the feminist and film literature to provide a critical overview of the chosen films, with a view to establishing educational possibilities for the complex issues dealt with in this study.

(Lewis 1998)

Women, sport and the challenge of politics: a case study of the Women's Sports Foundation United Kingdom

This study traced the development of the Women's Sports Foundation (WSF) in Britain over its first eleven years of operation (1984–1994). With the exception of the Canadian Association for the Advancement of Women and Sport and Physical Activity (CAAWS), women's sports advocacy organisations are under-researched as a relatively new organisational form. They represent a significant development in the history of women's attempts at gaining greater access to the sportsworld and are an important subject of study as vehicles of change. My interest in researching the British WSF emerged from my experiences as a volunteer with the organisation; this also provided me with insights into organisational issues that warranted exploration. Feminist thinking was central to this project, informing the rationale, methodology and analysis. After presenting a chronology of the major events in the history of the WSF, issues relating to the following themes were discussed: (1) the connections between the WSF and feminism; (2) the politics of sexuality; and (3) dealing with differences among women. Over the duration of its history the WSF has moved away from philosophical origins influenced by radical feminism towards a closer alliance with the values and priorities of the sports establishment. Although this has enabled the WSF to develop closer relations with the structures of sport, it has also meant that the organisation's agenda has become greatly depoliticised. In effect, the WSF has moved from being a women's sports advocacy organisation to a women's sports development agency. The impact of these changes are discussed in terms of the three themes. This study argues that making a political analysis of sport is fundamental to challenging gender inequality. Understanding the ideological processes at work in sport enables connections to be made between women's disadvantage in sport and their subordinate position in wider social structures. It is suggested that the WSF's ability to perform its function as the national organisation representing women's interests in sport is closely tied to its ability to link women, sport and politics.

(Grace 1995)

Application: writing an Abstract

Ask your student to use the analyses of the above two texts as a framework for writing their own Abstract.

The language of Abstracts

Cooley and Lewkowicz (2003) discuss the use of verb tense in Abstracts. As they point out, there are two ways the student may view their Abstract: as a summary of their thesis or dissertation, or as a summary of the research that was carried out. The first of these will typically use the *present simple* tense (This thesis *examines* ...). The second will typically use the *past simple* tense (The study *revealed* that ...) and the *present perfect* tense (Previous research *has shown* that ...). Table 11.1 is a summary of these different tense uses, with examples taken from the previous Abstracts.

Application: the language of Abstracts

Ask your student to identify uses of the present simple, past simple and present perfect in the Abstracts shown above. Which orientation does each Abstract mostly take, a summary of the thesis, or a report on the research? Next ask your student to check their use of verb tenses in the Abstract they wrote so that it takes one or the other orientations described by Coley and Lewkowicz (2003).

Table 11.1 Use of verb tenses in thesis and dissertation Abstracts

Summary of the thesis	
Present simple	This thesis *examines* the articulations of gender, class, and race in a specific sample of films from the 1930s to the 1990s.
Report of the research	
Past simple	This study *traced* the development of the Women's Sports Foundation (WSF) in Britain over its first eleven years of operation (1984–1994).
Present perfect	The WSF *has moved* away from philosophical origins influenced by radical feminism towards a closer alliance with the values and priorities of the sports establishment.

Writing the Acknowledgments section

Hyland (2004b) has studied thesis and dissertation Acknowledgments in detail. His work has shown not only that there are typical ways in which these texts are organized but also how students use these texts to display their disciplinary membership and networks at the same time as they thank the people that helped them in their academic undertaking. As Hyland (2004b: 323) points out, these short and seemingly simple texts 'bridge the personal and the public, the social and the professional, and the academic and the moral'. Through these texts, students balance debts and responsibilities at the same time as giving their readers 'a glimpse of a writer enmeshed in a network of personal and academic relationships'. The following is an example of how one of the students in Hyland's study expressed gratitude in their Acknowledgements section.

> The writing of an MA thesis is not an easy task. During the time of writing I received support and help from many people. In particular, I am profoundly indebted to my supervisor, Dr James Fung, who was very generous with his time and knowledge and assisted me in each step to complete the thesis. I am grateful to The School of Humanities and Social Sciences of HKUST whose research travel grant made the field work possible. Many thanks also to those who helped arrange the field work for me. And finally, but not least, thanks go to my whole family who have been an important and indispensable source of spiritual support. However, I am the only person responsible for errors in the thesis.
>
> (Hyland 2004b: 309)

In this Acknowledgements section, the student shows disciplinary membership and allegiances at the same time as thanking people for their support. The Acknowledgement observes appropriate academic values of modesty ('The writing of an MA thesis is not an easy task'), gratitude ('I am profoundly indebted to', 'I am grateful to', 'Many thanks to', etc.) and self-effacement ('I am the only person responsible for errors in the thesis'). These texts, thus, play important social and interpersonal roles in the thesis and dissertation writing process.

Hyland points out that there are typically three stages in Acknowledgements sections: a *reflecting move* which makes some introspective comment on the writer's research experience, a *thanking move* which gives credit to individuals and institutions, and an *announcing move* which accepts responsibility for any flaws or errors and dedicates the thesis to an individual or individual/s. Examples of each of these moves are shown in Table 11.2. Only the thanking move is obligatory in these texts, however, even though there are often more moves than this.

Table 11.2 Moves in Acknowledgements sections

Move	Examples
Reflecting move	The most rewarding achievement in my life, as I approach middle age, is the completion of my doctoral dissertation.
Thanking move Presenting participants	I would like to take this opportunity to express my immense gratitude to all those persons who have given their invaluable support and assistance.
Thanking for academic assistance, intellectual support, ideas, analyses, feedback, etc.	In particular, I am profoundly indebted to my supervisor, Dr James Fung, who was very generous with his time and knowledge and assisted me in each step to complete the thesis.
Thanking for resources, data access and clerical, technical and financial support, etc.	The research for this thesis was financially supported by a postgraduate studentship from the University of Hong Kong, The Hong Kong and China Gas Company Postgraduate Scholarship, Epson Foundation Scholarship, two University of Hong Kong CRCG grants and an RCG grant.
Thanking for moral support, friendship, encouragement, sympathy, patience, etc.	I'd include those who helped including my supervisor, friends, and colleagues. It is also appropriate to thank for spiritual support, so I'd also include my friends in church and family members.
Announcing move Accepting responsibility for flaws or errors	Notwithstanding all of the above support for this project, any errors and/or omissions are solely my own.
Dedicating the thesis to an individual/s	I love my family. This thesis is dedicated to them.

Source: based on Hyland 2004b

Application: analysing a sample Acknowledgements section

Ask your student to analyse the structure of the following Acknowledgements section and identify the ways in which the writer has expressed gratitude to the people that helped her with her thesis.

I am deeply indebted to my thesis advisor Elizabeth Wood, who approved my topic, edited my thesis and gave me invaluable advice both in person and on the phone. I would also like to thank her for her wit, humanity and constant encouragement of my endeavours. She is truly an inspired soul.

I would also like to extend thanks to the faculty members of the Department of Cultures and Values for their generosity, especially Dr David Smith, Grace Wong-McAllister, Dr Ratna Ghosh and Dr Bill Lawlor, whose magical presence I miss tremendously.

Special thanks is reserved for my father, who helped me gather several of my references when I sat on many library floors on the verge of frustration and for just being there. In addition, I am indebted to my younger brother, Atiba Lewis, whose extensive computer skills saved me on several occasions.

* This thesis is dedicated to the memory of Frances Falmer.

(Lewis 1998)

Application: writing Acknowledgements

Ask your student to use their analysis of the above text as a framework for writing their Acknowledgements section.

Conclusion

The Abstract and Acknowledgements sections are, thus, short but important pieces of text. They orient the reader to what the student has done as well as where the student is placed in various scholarly and social networks. These seemingly simple texts need as much attention as other parts of student's text. Like the table of contents, the Abstract and Acknowledgements sections are often the last thing a student writes, but among the first things an examiner reads. As Finn (2005: 118) argues, 'first impressions last' in the examination process. Clear and well-written Abstracts and Acknowledgements sections can help make that first impression a good one.

Chapter 12

Resources for thesis and dissertation writing

A quick internet search will reveal thousands of resources on thesis and dissertation writing in book and online formats. The resources described here are those that we use ourselves and recommend to our students; they have a focus on writing rather than on general tips for completing a PhD or a master's degree.

Theses and dissertations online

- *UMI ProQuest dissertations and theses.* This extensive online database includes the majority of doctoral dissertations and master's theses submitted at US universities, available in PDF formats. Most university libraries should have a subscription. This database is an excellent resource, particularly, but not solely, for those writing a North American PhD or master's thesis. Users can sign up for email alerts to keep abreast of developments in their field. More information is available on the ProQuest website, available online at: <http://www.proquest.com/products_umi/dissertations/> (accessed 8 September 2006).
- *The Australian digital thesis program.* Copies of many recent Australian PhD theses in PDF files are available in a searchable database. This open-access repository enables new students to gain a sense of what a completed thesis in their field 'looks like'. Available online at: <http://adt.caul.edu.au/> (accessed 9 September 2006).

Thesis and dissertation writing websites

- Azuma, R.T. *So long, and thanks for the Ph.D.!* A computer science PhD student's guide to surviving graduate school. Everything he wishes he had known when he started out. Very useful for students in engineering fields in general, with humour added and the wisdom of hindsight. Available online at: <http://www.cs.unc.edu/~azuma/hitch4.html> (accessed 9 September 2006).
- *Creating your thesis with Microsoft Word.* Many of the features of MSWord can help with managing and organizing a long document such as a thesis. This

site provides a thesis template and tips on how to use those features of Word that can help structure a thesis. Available online at: < http:// ist. uwaterloo.ca/ew/thesis/Thesis_word.html> (accessed 7 September 2006).

- *Getting started on your literature review.* A useful overview for students in the early stages of thesis writing. Available online at: <http://www.lc. unsw.edu.au/onlib/litrev.html> (accessed 8 September 2006).

- Levine, S.J. *Writing and presenting your thesis or dissertation.* A very comprehensive and accessible, easy-to-navigate site with a student focus, written by an experienced supervisor. The emphasis is on strategies that will help successful writing and completion. Much sound advice for the supervisor too. Available online at: <http://www.learnerassociates.net/dissthes/> (accessed 8 September 2006).

- *PhD web – first thoughts to finished writing.* A highly recommended website. Its comprehensive 'Frequently Asked Questions' are an excellent resource for student and supervisor as are the sections on managing the different stages of the PhD. Good hyperlinks make the site easy to navigate. Available online at: <http://www.sss.uq.edu.au/linkto/phdwriting/> (accessed 8 September 2006).

- *Re-envisioning the PhD.* This site, hosted by the University of Washington, was the outcome of a funded project which looked at re-envisioning the PhD to meet the societal needs of the twenty-first century. The section on PhD resources provides a useful portal to lots of interesting links. Available online at: <http://www.grad.washington.edu/envision/index.html> (accessed 9 September 2006).

- *Resources for postgraduates.* A useful portal with links to a wide range of online resources on topics such as 'What makes a good PhD', 'Choosing a research topic', 'Organising your ideas', and 'Managing your time'. Available online at: <http://www.slc.auckland.ac.nz/resources/for_postgraduates/index.php> (accessed 9 September 2006).

- *Thesis proposals: a brief guide.* A concise handout on the topic for students in the proposal writing stage. Available online at: <http://www.lc.unsw.edu.au/onlib/thesis.html> (accessed 9 September 2006).

- Wolfe, J. *How to write a PhD thesis.* Although initially written for PhD students in physics, students from a range of scientific disciplines have found this website's tips on getting started and organized, finding a structure and dividing the task into less formidable pieces a valuable resource. Available online at: <http://www.phys.unsw.edu.au/~jw/thesis.html#start> (accessed 9 September 2006).

Online writing support

- *Academic grammar for students of the Arts and Social Sciences.* This site is aimed at the second-language student and provides very helpful resources on academic writing, writing a literature review and writing research proposals.

Available online at: <http://ecdev.hku.hk/acadgrammar/> (accessed 17 August 2006).

- *Writing up research.* This resource is intended primarily for master's degree students starting their research writing, but could be a useful starting point to any second-language student writer commencing postgraduate study. Available online at: <http://www.clet.ait.ac.th/EL21OPEN. HTM> (accessed 9 September 2006).
- This resource is complemented by an open-access online course entitled *Writing up research.* Available online at: <http://www.clet.ait.ac.th/Wur/content.htm> (accessed 9 September 2006).
- *Analysis of academic English.* A vocabulary-building website that draws on the latest concordancing technology to help students to develop their academic vocabulary. Available online at: <http://ec.hku.hk/vec/concord/index.htm> (accessed 9 September 2006).

Books on thesis and dissertation writing

We have found the following books useful for teaching thesis and dissertation writing. Some of these books discuss language features of academic writing, while others focus more on aspects of carrying out, and writing up, research.

- Bailey 2006: this excellent book has chapters on many of the language issues with which second-language students have difficulty in academic writing, such as paraphrasing, referencing, using referring verbs and the use of articles. Each section has exercises with an answer key for each of the exercises. If your student wants a book to help them with their English, this is one of the best there is.
- Boddington and Clanchy 1999: a very clear, well-laid-out guide to the more advanced reading skills needed by the postgraduate student in an English-medium environment.
- Booth *et al.* 1995: this book goes through each of the stages of the research process, from finding a topic through to generating research questions, constructing arguments, planning, organizing, drafting and revising chapters, through to writing a thesis that meets the needs of the community of readers at which it is aimed.
- Craswell 2005: while aimed at academic writing in general, this book has sections on thesis writing that cover a lot of key areas. There are also chapters on managing academic writing, the mechanics of academic writing, writing a literature review and other academic texts such as journal articles and books.
- Dunleavy 2003: Patrick Dunleavy shares his accumulated wisdom as an experienced doctoral supervisor and academic writer in the social sciences. Focusing on the links between writing and thinking, his book takes the student through the process of planning, drafting, writing,

revising and shaping the thesis in an engaging, insightful and some-times amusing way.

- Elphinstone and Schweitzer 1998: this small but comprehensive volume should be required reading for all commencing postgraduate research students and their supervisors. It is one of the best there is.
- Evans and Gruba 2002: a highly recommended, easily accessible and comprehensive guide that focuses on writing the various sections of the thesis based on the writers' extensive experience of supervising and sup-porting students. Its specific Australian focus does not make it any less applicable internationally.
- Hart 1998: a key text that all students in the social sciences should be familiar with before starting their literature review.
- Hart 2005: a thorough and comprehensive handbook aimed at support-ing students doing a master's dissertation in the social sciences. It has sections on formulating a topic and finding a format, on research design and methodology, on ethics and a final section on writing.
- Holliday 2002: although not specifically aimed at doctoral or master's students, this book is one of the few that help qualitative researchers understand that the writing process is an integral part of doing qualita-tive research and becoming a qualitative researcher. It considers the particular challenges confronting qualitative writers as they attempt to 'find their voice'.
- Kamler and Thomson 2006: this innovative book offers all those supervi-sors who struggle to help their doctoral students with their writing powerful strategies for understanding the ways in which language and grammar can be put to work to assist novice writers develop their iden-tity as a scholarly writer. Mini case studies of their own students' writing dilemmas and suggested solutions enliven the text.
- Madsen 1992: Madsen's book has sections on selecting and shaping a research topic, preparing the research proposal, organizing writing and adapting the thesis for publication and presentation. The appendix con-tains several sample research proposals.
- Manolo and Trafford 2004: this book covers many key issues for research students such as time- and self-management and making the most of available resources. There is also a very useful chapter on writing a high quality thesis or dissertation.
- Meloy 1994: this book examines the experiences of a number of students writing a qualitative dissertation in the areas of communication, educa-tion, geology, nursing and sociology. There are many personal experiences in the book that qualitative dissertation writers will relate to.
- Murray 2002: one of the few books that actually takes student writers through the process of writing a thesis at the various stages of the PhD. It cannot be recommended too highly. It is a book to be dipped into again

and again depending on the particular problem encountered and will prove an invaluable source of inspiration and encouragement.

- Phillips and Pugh 2005: this book covers issues such as the PhD process, the nature of the PhD, what students expect from their supervisors, university responsibilities and departmental responsibilities. There is a summary of the contents of the second edition of this book available online at: <http://www.csis.hku.hk/~ehung/phdhandbook/phdhandbook.htm> (accessed 9 September 2006).

- Rudestam and Newton 2001: still one of the better comprehensive guides around with really useful sections on the different components of the thesis and how to conceptualize and present them. The chapters on writing are particularly worthwhile. Students love the 'Twelve tricks to keep you going when you write'.

- Swales and Feak 1994; second edition 2004: this seminal text aimed at non-native speakers writing at a postgraduate level is highly recommended. Its explicit and accessible focus on language and writing make it an essential item for students' bookshelves and for supervisors wanting to understand more about how academic discourse functions.

- Swales and Feak 2000: this volume by Swales and Feak has many chapters that are useful for research students, such as writing literature reviews; writing the thesis abstract; writing the acknowledgements and the final chapter; and applying for academic positions. There are also sections on other genres such as conference abstracts and poster presentations.

- Wallace and Wray 2006: aimed specifically at postgraduate students in the social sciences, this new guide should be very useful to students and supervisors working to develop the habits and skills of reading critically and becoming a self-critical writer. The final section of the book focuses on building a critical literature review and integrating it into a thesis or dissertation.

- Zerubavel 1999: *The Clockwork Muse* provides a way through 'writer's block' via an examination of the writing practices of successful writers. It challenges the romantic ideal of the inspired writer dashing off a piece of writing when the 'muse' descends. Instead, writers are offered a simple yet comprehensive framework that considers such variables as when to write, for how long, and how often, while keeping a sense of momentum throughout the entire project. Routines and regularities facilitate 'inspiration'.

Appendix

A sample research proposal

Two aspects of Japanese sentence final expressions in relation to gender: expressing modality and constructing stereotypes

Summary of the research

This project examines the speech of Japanese women and men. Japanese is known to exhibit different speech styles between women and men, which is most apparent in the choice of sentence ending form. This form can indicate the gender of the speaker as well as the attitude of the speaker. The literature suggests that male ending choices are often perceived as sounding vulgar and enforcing solidarity; therefore, women are not expected to use these forms. On the other hand, female ending choices are polite, indirect, less assertive, and soft sounding. These features, especially the lack of assertiveness, encourage the addressees participating in the conversation, allowing the conversation to be carried out cooperatively.

As some of these ending forms strongly suggest femininity or masculinity, they are often used to depict stereotypical women and men. These endings are found in all manner of scripted conversations as well as very casual conversation-style writing, such as novels, film scripts, advertisements and magazine articles. In those written conversations, women are consistently enforcing their femininity and men their masculinity with the ending forms. However, according to recent studies, gender-related forms are not used as frequently in actual conversation as they are seen in written texts, and some are even disappearing. Moreover, cross-gender usage has been observed.

This project will investigate the current usage of the gender-related forms by young Japanese women and men, in particular, the function, frequency and circumstance of occurrence of each ending form. Differences between actual language use and the speech style in a planned (scripted) conversation will be discussed including the style employed when quoting others. Then these conversation styles will be compared to determine the gender identity in Japanese culture presented by the different speech style.

Purpose of the research

The purpose of the research is to clarify the function of gender-related sentence final expressions, including particles, copulas and morphemes attached to verbs. Instead of describing the normative use of these expressions, the proposed study intends to observe how they are actually used by whom and in which context. Then the study will discuss how these expressions are used to construct stereotypes of women and men.

Relevant background literature

Japanese women's language attracted people's attention when Akiko Jugaku published *Onna to Nihongo* (Women and Japanese) in 1979. Since then, similar to the development of research on women's language in English, both a 'difference' approach and a 'dominance' approach has been taken.

Sachiko Ide is playing the leading role in the 'difference' approach and argues that language difference between men and women comes from gender role difference rather than the result of men's dominance. Her interpretation is that women tend to spend more time on socializing with other women, which requires polite forms, while men spend more time at work where they need an efficient language. She also claims that women use women's language in order to keep their identity. Not only polite expressions but women's whole language function as equipment to create identity as an woman. Ide's position is that women are labelling themselves as women by choosing this feminine language.

The 'Dominance' approach is most obvious in Katsue Akiba Reynolds' (1991) work. She claims that the difference between women's and men's language today reflects the Japanese society of the feudal era in which women were viewed as second-class citizens. Although the social structure has changed, the culture which considers that women should be submissive and should talk accordingly has not changed. Keiko Abe (1990) focused on politeness differences and discovered that women's greetings are regarded as less polite when a man and a woman use the same greeting at work. In other words, women are expected to be more polite than men.

As for sentence final particles (SFP), two methods have been taken. One is an attempt to clarify their function and the reasons why women can use a certain set of particles and men cannot and vice versa. Researchers involved in this task claim that particles used by men are assertive and imply that the speaker takes full responsibility for the statement (McGloin 1991). On the other hand, particles used by women are seen as a tool to avoid being assertive (Ide 1991; McGloin 1991) According to these researchers, women's lower status and men's dominance in society are responsible for the different language use. As the younger and the inferior are not allowed to talk in an assertive manner to their counterparts, women are not allowed to talk assertively.

The other approach is to observe the frequency of these particles in real conversation. Researchers engaged in this task record conversations of several people and count how many particles are used. Recent studies have all shown that particles strongly suggesting femininity are becoming less and less popular and that even some particles suggesting masculinity are being used by women (Okamoto 1995).

Research question/s

The aim of this project is to investigate the functions of Japanese sentence final particles and the way they contribute to marking the gender of a speaker. My hypothesis is that there is not much clear distinction between women's and men's actual speech in terms of particle use, but stereotypical women's and men's speech exists in Japanese society. What makes this stereotypical speech is the connection of some functions of these particles and the stereotypical image of women or men. In order to make this connection clear, the function of each particle should be made clear. The following are the questions to be asked:

- Why are particular sentence final expressions associated with gender? What are their functions?
- When and how are these sentence final expressions actually used? What are the effects of these expressions?
- Is there any agreement among Japanese speakers on the stereotypical use of these gender-related sentence final expressions? Is there any difference between the actual use of these sentence final expressions and the stereotypical use of them?

Definitions of terms

- *Sentence Final Expressions:* These include sentence final particles, copulas, and style markers such as masu forms.
- *Sentence Final Particles:* These are sometimes referred as inter-personal particles as they are used for smooth communication and are not directly related to the proposition or the message of the utterance. Some of them, specifically, *ne, yo, na,* and *sa* can be used in the middle of a sentence. In theory, they can be inserted after any word, or a particle, if a word is followed by a particle. In the present study, however, I will refer to them as sentence final particles as they are found most typically at the sentence final position and behave in the same way as other sentence final particles.
- *Gender:* Whereas sex is a biological term which refers to biological differences between male and female, gender is socially constructed in a given culture – the division of maleness and femaleness which is expected to coincide with the biological division. It also refers to psychological attributes of each division.

- *Femininity:* This comprises attributes that society expects women to have and demonstrate through appearance and behaviour. The term also refers to 'the other' as opposed to the norm, which is represented by masculinity. Lisa Tuttle (1987) explains this as the result of patriarchal tradition. As society has placed the male at the centre and made women outsiders, 'femininity is in opposition to whatever is considered to be important civilisation'. The present study is mainly concerned with the former aspect. It will, however, refer to the latter where appropriate.
- *Masculinity:* This comprises attributes that society expects men to have and demonstrate through appearance and behaviour.

Research methodology

1 Analysis of gender differences in created conversations such as those that appear in fiction, film scripts and drama scripts.
2 Investigation of Japanese people's overt views towards women's language through literature.
3 Analysis of natural conversations. The conversations will be recorded in Japan, mainly in the Tokyo area, in order to focus on language use in standard Japanese. As the interest of the study is in the current use of sentence final particles, not traditional or innovative use, the subjects will be aged between 20 and 40.

Anticipated problems and limitations

There are many variations in both oral and written forms of Japanese language according to the region, generation, education and so on. Since it is not realistic to cover all variations, this study is limited to the language use of working women and men in Tokyo, whose age is between 20 and 40. However, other variables such as occupation, position at work, and family background may affect the data.

Significance of the research

The present study proposes to analyse the use of particles in natural conversations, with the role in the discourse and the context taken into consideration. Previous studies, regardless of their approach, lack the viewpoint of discourse and the context in which each sentence is uttered. A language form that indicates the speaker's attitude should not be discussed only at sentence level. Another problem is the source of the data. In some studies, the sentences discussed are written by the researchers themselves. In other words, the researcher's judgment reflects their stereotype. Other studies use conversations from works of fiction as the subject of study. Written conversations will not be dealt with as if they were natural conversations because there is no real interaction involved and, again, the writer's stereotype plays a big role.

Ethical considerations

As recordings of natural conversations will be involved, informed consent needs to be obtained. Both oral and written explanation of the study will be given to the informants before the recording. A written form will be signed by the informant to allow the researcher to use the data.

Timetable for the research

(i)   Literature review
  - data collection from published material
  - preparation for fieldwork
(ii) Fieldwork in Japan
  - library research in Japan
  - transcription and data analysis
(iii) Interpretation and analysis

Resources required for the research

- a tape recorder
- a video player
- a transcriber
- computer software for quantitative and qualitative analysis

Budget costs (for fieldwork)

- air fare to Japan
- insurance
- living costs
- audio/video tapes
- photocopying
- payment of participants

References

Abe, Keiko (1990) Data ni miru gendai no onna kotoba no sitai. *Monthly Japanese*, 2: 7–11.
Brown, Penelope (1998) How and why are women more polite: some evidence from a Mayan community. In J. Coates (ed.) *Language and Gender*, London: Blackwell, 100–120.

Brown, Penelope and Stephen Levinson (1987) *Politeness: Some Universals in Language Usage*, Cambridge: Cambridge University Press.

Cameron, Deborah (ed.) (1990) *The Feminist Critique of Language*, London: Routledge.

Cameron, Deborah (1991) *Feminism in Linguistic Theory*, London: Macmillan.

Coates, Jennifer (1986) *Women, Men and Language*, New York: Longman.

Coates, Jennifer (ed.) (1998) *Language and Gender*, London: Blackwell.

Cook, Haruko Minegishi (1990) The sentence-final particle ne as a tool for cooperation in Japanese conversation. In Hajime Hoji (ed.) *Japanese/Korean Linguistics*, Stanford: CSLI, 29–44.

Cook, Haruko Minegishi (1992) Meanings of non-referential indexes: a case study of the Japanese sentence-final particle *ne*, *Text*, 12 (4): 507–539.

Eckert, Penelope and Sally McConnell-Ginet (1998) Communities of practice: where language, gender, and power all live. In J. Coates (ed.) *Language and Gender*, London: Blackwell, 484–494.

Gal, Suzan (1995) Language, gender, and power: an anthropological review. In Kira Hall and Mary Bucholts (eds) *Gender Articulated: Language and the Socially Constructed Self*, New York: Routledge, 169–182.

Ide, Sachiko (1982) Japanese sociolinguistics: politeness and women's language. *Lingua* 57, 57–385.

Ide, Sachiko, Motoko Hori, Akiko Kawasaki, Shoko Ikuta and Hitomi Haga (1986) Sex difference and politeness in Japanese. *International Journal of Society and Language*, 58: 25–36.

Ide, Sachiko (1991) How and why do women speak more politely in Japanese. In Sachiko Ide and Naomo Hanaoka-McGloin (eds) *Aspects of Japanese Women's Language*, Tokyo: Kuroshio Shuppan, 63–79.

Ide, Sachiko and Naomi Hanaoka McGloin (eds) (1991) *Aspect of Japanese Women's Language*, Tokyo: Kuroshio Shuppan.

Jugaku, Akiko (1979) *Onna to Nihongo* (Japanese and Women), Tokyo: Iwanami Shoten.

Labov, William (1972) *Sociolinguistic Patterns*, Philadelphia: University of Pennsylvania Press.

Lakoff, Robin (1975) *Language and Woman's Place*, New York: Harper & Row.

Lipman, Walter (1922) *Public Opinion*, London: Macmillan.

McGloin, Naomi Hanaoka (1991) Sex difference and sentence-final particles. In Sachiko Ide and Naomo Hanaoka McGloin (eds), *Aspects of Japanese Women's Language*, Tokyo: Kuroshio Shuppan, 23–42.

Maynard, Senko (1991) Pragmatics of discourse modality: a case of *da* and *desu/masu* forms in Japanese, *Journal of Pragmatics*, 15: 551–582.

Maynard, Senko (1993) *Discourse Modality: Subjectivity, Emotion and Voice in the Japanese Language*, Philadelphia: John Benjamins Publishing Company.

Milroy, Lesley (1987) *Observing and Analysing Natural Language: A Critical Account of Sociolinguistic Method*, London: Basil Blackwell.

Mizutani, Osamu and Nobuko Mizutani (1987) *How to Be Polite in Japanese*, Tokyo: The Japan Times.

Ochs, Elinor (1993) Indexing gender. In Barbara Diane Miller (ed) *Sex and Gender Hierarchies*, Cambridge: Cambridge University Press, 146–69.

Okamoto, Shigeko (1995) 'Tasteless' Japanese: Less 'feminine' speech among young Japanese women. In Kira Hall and Mary Bucholts (eds) *Gender Articulated: Language and the Socially Constructed Self*, New York: Routledge, 297–325.

Okamoto, Shigeko (1997) Social context, linguistic ideology, and indexical expressions in Japanese, *Journal of Pragmatics*, 8: 795–817.

Reynolds, Katsue Akiba (1991) Female speakers of Japanese in transition. In S. Ide and N. H. McGloin (eds) *Aspects of Japanese Women's Language*, Tokyo: Kurosio Publishers, 129–146.

Shibamoto, Janet S. (1985) *Japanese Women's Language*, Orlando: Academic Press.

Trudgill, Peter (1972) Sex, covert prestige and linguistic change in the urban British English of Norwich. *Language in Society*, 1: 179–195.

Trudgill, Peter (1974) *The Social Differentiation of English in Norwich*, Cambridge: Cambridge University Press.

Tuttle, Lisa (1987) *Encyclopedia of Feminism*, London: Arrow Books.

Usami, Mayumi (1995) Conditions for speech-level shift occurrence in Japanese discourse, *Gakuen*, 662: 27–42.

Uchida, Akiko (1992) When 'difference' is 'dominance': a critique of the 'anti-power-based' cultural approach to sex differences, *Language in Society*, 21: 547–568.

References

Abasi, A.R., Akbari, N. and Graves, B. (2006) 'Discourse appropriation, construction of identities, and the complex issue of plagiarism: ESL students writing in graduate school', *Journal of Second Language Writing*, 15: 102–117.

Adams, K. and Cargill, M. (2003) 'Knowing that the other knows: using experience and reflection to enhance communication in cross-cultural postgraduate supervisory relationships', Proceedings of HERDSA Conference, Christchurch, July. Available online at: <http://surveys.canterbury.ac.nz/herdsa03/pdfsref/Y1001.pdf> (accessed 17 January 2006).

Allison, D., Cooley, L., Lewkowicz, J. and Nunan, D. (1998) 'Dissertation writing in action: the development of a dissertation writing support program for ESL graduate research students', *English for Specific Purposes*, 17: 199–217.

Al-Sharideh, K. and Goe, W.R. (1998) 'Ethnic communities within the university: an examination of factors influencing the personal adjustment of international students', *Research in Higher Education*, 39: 699–725.

Amy, S.W. (2000) 'A radio study of selected regions in the Magellanic Clouds', unpublished PhD thesis, University of Sydney. Available online at: <http://adt.library.usyd.edu.au/~thesis/adt-NU/public/adt-NU20010524.163700/> (accessed 12 September 2006).

Andrews, K.T. (1997) '"Freedom is a constant struggle": the dynamics and consequences of the Mississippi Civil Rights Movement, 1960–1984', unpublished PhD dissertation, State University of New York at Stony Brook.

Angelova, M. and Riazantseva, A. (1999) '"If you don't tell me, how can I know?": A case study of four international students learning to write the U.S. way', *Written Communication*, 16: 491–525.

Aspland, T. (1999) '"You learn round and I learn square": Mei's story', in Y. Ryan and O. Zuber-Skerrit (eds) *Supervising Postgraduates from Non-English Speaking Backgrounds*, Buckingham: Society for Research into Higher Education and the Open University Press.

Atkinson, D. (1997) 'Teaching and researching the thesis/dissertation in ESP', colloquium introduction at TESOL convention, Orlando, Florida, March.

Atkinson, D. and Curtis, A. (1998) *A Handbook for Postgraduate Researchers*, Hong Kong: Department of English, Hong Kong Polytechnic University.

Bailey, S. (2003) *Academic Writing: A Practical Guide for Students*, London: RoutledgeFalmer.

Bailey, S. (2006) *Academic Writing: A Handbook for International Students*, Abingdon: Routledge.

Ballard, B. and Clanchy, J. (1984) *Study Abroad: A Manual for Asian Students*, Selangor Darul Ehsan: Longman Malaysia.

Ballard, B. and Clanchy, J. (1997) *Teaching International Students: A Brief Guide for Lecturers and Supervisors*, Deakin, ACT: IDP Education Australia.

Banerjee, J. (2003) 'Interpreting and Using Proficiency Test Scores', unpublished thesis, Lancaster University.

Bartolome, L. (1998) *The Misteaching of Academic Discourses: The Politics of Language in the Classroom*, Boulder, CO: Westview Press.

Basturkman, H. and Bitchener, J. (2005) 'The text and beyond: exploring the expectations of the academic community for the discussion of results section in masters theses', *New Zealand Studies in Applied Linguistics*, 11: 1–19.

Becher, T. and Trowler, P.R. (2001) *Academic Tribes and Territories: Intellectual Enquiry and the Culture of Disciplines*, 2nd edn, Buckingham, UK: Open University Press.

Belcher, D. (1994) 'The apprenticeship approach to advanced academic literacy: graduate students and their mentors', *English for Specific Purposes*, 13: 23–34.

Belcher, D. and Hirvela, A. (2005) 'Writing the qualitative dissertation: what motivates and sustains a fuzzy genre?', *Journal of English for Academic Purposes*, 4: 187–205.

Bell, J. (1999) *Doing Your Research Project: A Guide for First-time Researchers in Education and Social Science*, 3rd edn, Buckingham: Open University Press.

Biggs, J., Lai, P., Tang, C. and Lavelle, E. (1999) 'Teaching writing to ESL graduate students: a model and an illustration', *British Journal of Educational Psychology*, 69: 293–306.

Bitchener, J. and Basturkman, H. (2006) 'Perceptions of the difficulties of postgraduate L2 thesis students writing the discussion section', *Journal of English for Academic Purposes*, 5: 4–18.

Boddington, P. and Clanchy, J. (1999) *Reading for Study and Research*, Melbourne: Longman.

Booth, W.C., Colomb. G.G. and Williams, J.M. (1995) *The Craft of Research*, Chicago: University of Chicago Press.

Bradley, G. (2000) 'Responding effectively to the mental health needs of international students', *Higher Education*, 30: 417–433.

Braine, G. (2002) 'Academic literacy and the nonnative speaker graduate student', *Journal of English for Academic Purposes*, 1: 59–68.

Brett, P. (1994) 'A genre analysis of the results sections of sociology articles', *English for Specific Purposes*, 13: 47–59.

Brookes, A. and Grundy, P. (1990) *Writing for Study Purposes*, Cambridge: Cambridge University Press.

Bryce, M. (2003) 'Defining the doctorate with Asian research students', Proceedings of Australian Association for Research in Education (AARE), Newcastle mini-conference. Available online at: <www.aare.edu.au/conf03nc/br03015z.pdf> (accessed 12 January 2006).

Bunton, D. (1999) 'The use of higher level metatext in PhD theses', *English for Specific Purposes*, 18: S41–S56.

Bunton, D. (2002) 'Generic moves in PhD thesis introductions', in J. Flowerdew (ed.) *Academic Discourse*, London: Longman.

Bunton, D. (2005) 'The structure of PhD conclusions chapters', *Journal of English for Academic Purposes*, 4: 207–224.

Cadman, K. (1997) 'Thesis writing for international students: a question of identity?' *English for Specific Purposes*, 16: 3–14.

Cadman, K. (2000) '"Voices in the Air": evaluations of the learning experiences of international postgraduates and their supervisors', *Teaching in Higher Education*, 5: 475–491.

Cadman, K. (2002) 'English for academic possibilities: the research proposal as a contested site in postgraduate pedagogy', *Journal of English for Academic Purposes*, 1: 85–104.

Cadman, K. (2005) 'Towards a "pedagogy of connection" in critical research education: a REAL story', *Journal of English for Academic Purposes*, 4: 353–367.

Caffarella, R.S. and Barnett, B.G. (2000) 'Teaching doctoral students to become scholarly writers: the importance of giving and receiving critiques', *Studies in Higher Education*, 25: 39–52.

Cahill, D. (1999) 'Contrastive rhetoric, orientalism, and the Chinese second language writer', unpublished PhD dissertation, University of Illinois at Chicago.

Canagarajah, A.S. (2002) *Critical Academic Writing and Multilingual Students*, Ann Arbor: University of Michigan Press.

Cargill, M. (1998) 'Cross-cultural postgraduate supervision meetings as intercultural communication', in M. Kiley and G. Mullins (eds) *Quality in Postgraduate Research: Managing the New Agenda*, Adelaide: University of Adelaide, Adelaide. Available online at: <http://www.qpr.edu.au/1998/cargill98.pdf> (accessed 12 January 2006).

Cargill, M. (2000) 'Intercultural postgraduate supervision meetings: an exploratory discourse study', *Prospect*, 15: 28–38.

Casanave, C.P. (1995) 'Local interactions: constructing contexts for composing in a graduate sociology program', in D. Belcher and G. Braine (eds) *Academic Writing in a Second Language: Essays on Research and Pedagogy*, Norwood, NJ: Ablex.

Casanave, C.P. (2002) *Writing Games: Multicultural Case Studies of Academic Literacy Practices in Higher Education*, Mahwah: NJ: Laurence Erlbaum.

Charney, D.H. and Carlson, R.A. (1995) 'Learning to write in a genre: what student writers take from model texts', *Research in the Teaching of English*, 29: 88–125.

Coffin, C. (2000) 'History as discourse: construals of time, cause and appraisal', unpublished PhD thesis, University of New South Wales. Available online at: http://www.library.unsw.edu.au/~thesis/adt-NUN/public/adt-NUN20010920.110615/> (accessed 27 May 2006).

Cone, J.D. and Foster, S.L. (1993) *Dissertations and Theses: From Start to Finish*, Washington, DC: American Psychological Association.

Cooley, L. and Lewkowicz, J. (2003) *Dissertation Writing in Practice: Turning Ideas into Text*, Hong Kong: Hong Kong University Press.

Craswell, G. (2005) *Writing for Academic Success: A Postgraduate Guide*, London: Sage.

Cryer, P. and Okorocha, E. (1999) 'Avoiding potential pitfalls in the supervision of NESB students', in Y. Ryan and O. Zuber-Skerrit (eds) *Supervising Postgraduates from Non-English Speaking Backgrounds*, Buckingham, UK: Society for Research into Higher Education and the Open University Press.

Dahl, T. (2004) 'Textual metadiscourse in research articles: a marker of national culture or of academic discipline?' *Journal of Pragmatics*, 36: 1807–1825.

Davis, G.B and Parker, C.A. (1997) *Writing the Doctoral Dissertation: A Systematic Approach*, 2nd edn, Woodbury, NY: Barron's Educational Series.

Dedrick, R.F. and Watson, F. (2002) 'Mentoring needs of female, minority and international graduate students: a content analysis of academic research guides and related print material', *Mentoring & Tutoring*, 10: 275–289.

Deem, R. and Brehony, K.J. (2000) 'Doctoral students' access to research cultures – are some more unequal than others?' *Studies in Higher Education*, 25: 149–165.

Delamount, S., Atkinson, P. and Parry, O. (1997) *Supervising the PhD: A Guide to Success*, Buckingham, UK: Society for Research into Higher Education and Open University Press.

Dong, Y.R. (1997) 'Supervising international students requires cultural sensitivity', *The Scientist*, 11 (19): 10.

Dong, Y.R. (1998) 'Non-native speaker graduate students' thesis/dissertation writing in science: self-reports by students and their advisors from two U.S. institutions', *English for Specific Purposes*, 17: 369–390.

Dudley-Evans, T. (1986) 'Genre analysis: an investigation of the introduction and discussion sections of MSc dissertations', in M. Coulthard (ed.) *Talking about Text*, Birmingham, UK: University of Birmingham.

Dudley-Evans, T. (1993) 'Variation in communication patterns between discourse communities: the case of highway engineering and plant biology', in G. Blue (ed.) *Language Learning and Success: Studying through English*, London: Macmillan.

Dudley-Evans, T. (1997) 'Genre models for the teaching of academic writing to second language speakers: advantages and disadvantages', in T. Miller (ed.) *Functional Approaches to Written Text: Classroom Applications*, Washington, DC: United States Information Agency.

Dudley-Evans, T. (1999) 'The dissertation: a case of neglect?' in P. Thompson (ed.) *Issues in EAP Writing Research and Instruction*, Reading, UK: Centre for Applied Language Studies, University of Reading.

Dunleavy, P. (2003) *Authoring a PhD: How to Plan, Draft, Write and Finish a Doctoral Thesis or Dissertation*, Hampshire, UK: Palgrave Macmillan.

Elphinstone, L. and Schweitzer, R. (1998) *How to Get a Research Degree: A Survival Guide*, St Leonards, NSW: Allen and Unwin.

Epps, J. (2000) 'Wideband extension of narrowband speech for enhancement and coding', unpublished PhD thesis, University of Sydney.

Evans, D. and Gruba, P. (2002) *How to Write a Better Thesis*, Carlton South, Vic: Melbourne University Press.

Finn, J.A. (2005) *Getting a PhD. An Action Plan to Help Manage your Research, your Supervisor and Your Project.* London: Routledge.

Flowerdew, J. (1993) 'An educational, or process, approach to the teaching of professional genres', *ELT Journal*, 47: 305–316.

Flowerdew, J. (1999) 'Problems in writing for scholarly publications in English: the case of Hong Kong', *Journal of Second Language Writing*, 8: 243–264.

Frost, A. (1999) 'Supervision of NESB postgraduate students in science-based disciplines', in Y. Ryan and O. Zuber-Skerrit (eds) *Supervising Postgraduates from Non-English Speaking Backgrounds*, Buckingham, UK: Society for Research into Higher Education and Open University Press.

Geake, J. and Maingard, C. (1999) 'NESB postgraduate students in a new university: plus ça change, plus c'est la même chose', in Y. Ryan and O. Zuber-Skerrit (eds) *Supervising Postgraduates from Non-English Speaking Backgrounds*, Buckingham, UK: Society for Research into Higher Education and Open University Press.

Grace, B.M. (1995) 'Women, sport and the challenge of politics: a case study of the Women's Sports Foundation United Kingdom', unpublished MA thesis, University of Alberta, Canada.

Graddol, D. (1999) 'The decline of the native speaker', *AILA review*, 13: 57–68.

Grant, B. and Knowles, S. (2000) 'Flights of imagination: academic women be(com)ing writers', *International Journal for Academic Development*, 5: 6–19.

Hart, C. (1998) *Doing a Literature Review*, London: Sage.

Hart, C. (2005) *Doing your Masters Dissertation*, London: Sage.

Harwood, N. (2005) '"I hoped to counteract the memory problem, but I made no impact whatsoever": discussing methods in computing science using *I*', *English for Specific Purposes*, 24: 239–365.

Hasrati, M. (2005) 'Legitimate peripheral participation and supervising PhD students', *Studies in Higher Education*, 30: 557–570.

Hewings, M. (1993) 'The end! How to conclude a dissertation', in G. Blue (ed.) *Language, Learning and Success: Studying through English*, London: Modern English Publications in association with the British Council, Macmillan.

Hinds, J. (1987) 'Reader versus writer responsibility: a new typology' in U. Connor and R. Kaplan (eds) *Writing Across Languages: Analysis of L2 Text*, Reading, MA: Addison-Wesley.

Hirvela, A. and Belcher, D. (2001) 'Coming back to voice: the multiple voices and identities of mature multilingual writers', *Journal of Second Language Writing*, 10: 83–106.

Hockey, J. (1996) 'A contractual solution to problems in the supervision of PhD degrees in the UK', *Studies in Higher Education*, 21: 359–371.

Hodge, B. (1998) 'Monstrous knowledge: doing PhDs in the new humanities', in A. Lee and B. Green (eds) *Postgraduate Studies: Postgraduate Pedagogies*, Sydney: Centre for Language and Literacy, University of Technology, Sydney.

Holbrook, A., Bourke, S., Lovat, T. and Dally, K. (2004) 'Investigating PhD thesis examination reports', *International Journal of Educational Research*, 41: 98–120.

Holland, A. (1998) 'Saving the Aborigines, the white woman's crusade: a study of gender, race and the Australian frontier, 1920s–1960s', unpublished PhD thesis, University of New South Wales.

Holliday, A. (2002) *Doing and Writing Qualitative Research*, London: Sage.

Hoolihan, J.P. (2005) 'Biology of Arabian Gulf sailfish', unpublished PhD thesis, University of New South Wales. Available online at: <http://www.library.unsw.edu.au/~thesis/adt-NUN/public/adt-NUN20050607.184544/> (accessed 26 May 2006).

Hopkins, A. and Dudley-Evans, T. (1988) 'A genre-based investigation of the discussion section in articles and dissertations', *English for Specific Purposes*, 7: 113–122.

Huff, A.H. (1999) *Writing for Scholarly Publication*, Thousand Oaks, CA: Sage.

Humphrey, R. and McCarthy, P. (1999) 'Recognising difference: providing for postgraduate students', *Studies in Higher Education*, 24: 371–386.

Hyland, K. (1996) 'Talking to the academy: forms of hedging in science research articles', *Written Communication*, 13: 251–281.

Hyland, K. (1999) 'Talking to students: metadiscourse in introductory coursebooks', *English for Specific Purposes*, 18: 3–26.

Hyland, K. (2000) *Disciplinary Discourses: Social Interactions in Academic Writing*, London: Longman.

Hyland, K. (2002) 'Authority and invisibility: authorial identity in academic writing,' *Journal of Pragmatics*, 34: 1091–1112.

Hyland, K. (2004a) 'Disciplinary interactions: metadiscourse in L2 postgraduate writing,' *Journal of Second Language Writing*, 13: 133–151.

Hyland, K. (2004b) 'Graduates' gratitude: the generic structure of dissertation acknowledgements', *English for Specific Purposes*, 23: 303–324.

Hyland, K. (2005a) *Metadiscourse: Exploring Interaction in Writing*, London: Continuum.

Hyland, K. (2005b) 'Stance and engagement: a model of interaction in academic discourse', *Discourse Studies*, 7: 173–192.

Hyland, K. and Tse, P. (2004) 'Metadiscourse in academic writing: a reappraisal', *Applied Linguistics*, 25: 156–177.

Johns, A.M. (1990) 'L1 composition theories: implications for developing theories of L2 composition', in B. Kroll (ed.) *Second Language Writing: Research Insights for the Classroom*, Cambridge: Cambridge University Press.

Johns, A.M. (1995) 'Genre and pedagogical purposes', *Journal of Second Language Writing*, 4: 181–190.

Johns, A.M. and Swales, J.M. (2002) 'Literacy and disciplinary practices: opening and closing perspectives', *Journal of English for Academic Purposes*, 1: 13–28.

Johnston, S. (1997) 'Examining the examiners: an analysis of examiners' reports on doctoral theses', *Studies in Higher Education*, 22: 333–347.

Jones, A. (2001) 'Critical thinking, culture, and context: an investigation of teaching and learning in introductory macroeconomics', unpublished MEd thesis, University of Melbourne.

Kamler, B. and Thomson, P. (2006) *Helping Doctoral Students Write*, Abingdon: Routledge.

Kamler, B. and Threadgold, T. (1997) 'Which thesis did you read?' in Z. Golebiowski (ed.) *Policy and Practice of Tertiary Literacy*, Proceedings of the First National Conference on Tertiary Literacy: Research and Practice. Volume 1. Melbourne: Victoria University of Technology.

Kaplan, R.B. (1966) 'Cultural thought patterns in intercultural education', *Language Learning*, 16: 1–20.

Kiley, M. (1998) '"Expectation" in a cross-cultural postgraduate experience', in M. Kiley and G. Mullins (eds) *Quality in Postgraduate Research: Managing the New Agenda*, Adelaide: University of Adelaide. Available online at: <http://www.qpr.edu.au/1998/kiley1998.pdf> (accessed 17 January 2006).

Kiley, M. (2003) 'Conserver, strategist or transformer: the experience of postgraduate student sojourners', *Teaching in Higher Education*, 8: 345–356.

King, M. (1996) 'What examiners typically say', Presentation by Professor Mike King, Dean of Graduate Studies, Charles Sturt University.

Kubota, R. (1997) 'A reevaluation of the uniqueness of Japanese written discourse: implications for contrastive rhetoric', *Written Communication*, 14: 460–480.

Kubota, R. and Lehner, A. (2004) 'Toward critical contrastive rhetoric', *Journal of Second Language Writing*, 13: 7–27.

Lee, A. and Boud, D. (2003) 'Writing groups, change and academic identity research development as local practice', *Studies in Higher Education*, 28: 187–200.

Leki, I. (1997) 'Cross-talk: ESL issues and contrastive rhetoric', in C. Severino, J.C. Guerra and S.E. Butler (eds) *Writing in Multicultural Settings*, New York: Modern Language Association of America.

Levine S.J. (2002) *Writing and Presenting Your Thesis or Dissertation*. Available online at: <http://www.learnerassociates.net/dissthes/#29> (accessed 12 September 2006).

Lewis, A.G. (1998) 'The political and educational implications of gender, class and race in Hollywood film: holding out for a female hero', unpublished MA thesis, McGill University, Canada.

Lewis, M.F. (2000) 'The significance of episodic recharge in the wheatbelt of Western Australia', unpublished PhD thesis, University of Melbourne. Available online at: <http://eprints.unimelb.edu.au/archive/00000682/> (accessed 12 September 2006).

Liu, D. (2005) 'Plagiarism and ESOL students: is cultural conditioning truly the major culprit?' *ELT Journal*, 59: 234–241.

Locke, L.F., Spirduso, W.W and Silverman, S.S. (2000) *Proposals that Work: A Guide for Planning Dissertation and Grant Proposals*, 4th edn, Thousand Oaks, CA: Sage.

Madsen, D. (1992) *Successful Dissertations and Theses. A Guide to Graduate Student Research from Proposal to Completion*, 2nd edn, San Francisco: Jossey-Bass.

Manalo, E. and Trafford, J. (2004) *Thinking to Thesis: A Guide to Graduate Success at all Levels*, Auckland: Pearson Education.

Mauch, J.E. and Birch, J.W. (1998) *Guide to the Successful Thesis and Dissertations: A Handbook for Students and Faculty*, 4th edn, New York: Marcel Dekker.

Mauranen, A. (1993) 'Contrastive ESP rhetoric: metatext in Finnish-English economics text', *English for Specific Purposes*, 12: 3–22.

Medway, P. (2002) 'Fuzzy genres and community identities: the case of architecture students' sketchbooks', in R. Coe, L. Lingard and T. Teslenko (eds) *The Rhetoric and Ideology of Genre*, Cresskill, NJ: Hampton Press.

Meloy, J.M. (1994) *Writing the Qualitative Dissertation: Understanding by Doing*, Hillsdale, NJ: Lawrence Erlbaum.

Miles M.B. and Huberman A.M. (1994) *Qualitative Data Analysis: An Expanded Sourcebook*, Thousand Oaks, CA: Sage.

Moore, T. and Searcy, H. (1998) 'Theses and dissertations: a guided tour', in P. Master and D. Brinton (eds) *New Ways in English for Specific Purposes*, Alexandra, VA: TESOL.

Morley, L., Leonard, D. and David, M. (2002) 'Variation in vivas: quality and equality in British PhD assessments', *Studies in Higher Education*, 27: 263–273.

Morss, K. and Murray, R. (2001) 'Researching academic writing within a structured programme: insights and outcomes', *Studies in Higher Education*, 26: 35–51.

Moses, I. (1984) 'Supervision of higher degree students: problem areas and possible solutions', *Higher Education Research and Development*, 3: 153–165.

Moses, I. (1992) 'Role perception rating scale', in Ingrid Moses (ed.) *Research Training and Supervision: Proceedings from the ARC and AVCC sponsored conference*, Canberra: NBEET.

Mullins, G. and Kiley, M. (2002) '"It's a PhD, not a Nobel Prize": how experienced examiners assess research theses', *Studies in Higher Education*, 27: 369–386.

Murray, R. (2002) *How to Write a Thesis*, Buckingham, UK: Open University Press.

Murray, R. (2004) *Writing for Academic Journals*, Buckingham, UK: Open University Press.

Murray, R. (2005) 'What can I write about?: the rhetorical question for PhD students and their supervisors', *Working Papers on the Web*, 8. Available online at: <www.shu.ac.uk/wpw/supervision> (accessed 6 May 2006).

Myles, J. and Cheng, L. (2003) 'The social and cultural life of non-native English speaking international graduate students at a Canadian university', *Journal of English for Academic Purposes*, 2: 247–263.

Nagata, Y. (1999) '"Once I couldn't even spell PhD student, but now I *are* one!" Personal experiences of an NEB student', in Y. Ryan and O. Zuber-Skerrit (eds) *Supervising Postgraduates from Non-English Speaking Backgrounds*, Buckingham: Society for Research into Higher Education and Open University Press.

Norris, S.E. (2000) 'A parallel Navier-Stokes solver for natural convection and free surface flow', unpublished PhD thesis, University of Sydney. Available online at: <http://adt.library.usyd.edu.au/~thesis/adt-NU/public/adt-NU20010730.120215/> (accessed 12 September 2006).

Nunan, D. (1992) *Research Methods in Language Learning*, Cambridge: Cambridge University Press.

O'Shannessy, C. (1995) 'Pre-court barrister-client interactions: an investigation', unpublished MA thesis, University of Melbourne.

Paltridge, B. (1997) 'Thesis and dissertation writing: preparing ESL students for research', *English for Specific Purposes*, 16, 1: 61–70.

Paltridge, B. (2002) 'Thesis and dissertation writing: an examination of published advice and actual practice', *English for Specific Purposes*, 21: 125–143.

Paltridge, B. (2003) 'Teaching thesis and dissertation writing', *Hong Kong Journal of Applied Linguistics*, 8: 78–96.

Paltridge, B. (2006) *Discourse Analysis*, London: Continuum.

Parry, S. (1998) 'Disciplinary differences in doctoral theses', *Higher Education*, 36: 273–299.

Parry, S. and Hayden, M. (1996) 'The range of practices in higher degree supervision: disciplinary and organizational differences', paper presented at the 11th Vice-Chancellor's Forum on Teaching, University of Sydney, 17 May.

Pennycook, A. (1996) 'Borrowing others' words: text, ownership, memory, and plagiarism', *TESOL Quarterly*, 30: 201–230.

Pennycook, A. (2001) *Critical Applied Linguistics: A Critical Introduction*, Mahwah, NJ: Laurence Erlbaum.

Phillips, E.M. and Pugh, D.S. (2005) *How to Get a PhD*, 4th edn, Buckingham, UK: Open University Press.

Posteguillo, S. (1999) 'The schematic structure of computer science research articles', *English for Specific Purposes*, 18: 139–160.

Prince, A. (2000) 'Writing through cultures: the thesis writing experiences of five postgraduate research students from non-English speaking backgrounds and cultures', unpublished MA thesis, University of Melbourne.

Prior, P. (1995) 'Redefining the task: an ethnographic examination of writing and response in graduate seminars', in D. Belcher and G. Braine (eds) *Academic Writing in a Second Language: Essays in Research and Pedagogy*, Norwood: NJ: Ablex.

Prior, P. (1998) *Writing/disciplinarity*, Mahwah, NJ: Lawrence Erlbaum.

Riazi, A. (1997) 'Acquiring disciplinary literacy: a social-cognitive analysis of text production and learning among Iranian graduate students of education', *Journal of Second Language Writing*, 6: 105–137.

Richardson, L. (2000) 'Writing: a method of inquiry', in N. Denzin and Y. Lincoln (eds) *The Handbook of Qualitative Research*, Thousand Oaks, CA: Sage.

Robinson, C.R. (2002) 'Being somewhere: young homeless people in inner-city Sydney', unpublished PhD thesis, University of New South Wales.

Rudestam, K.E. and Newton, R.R. (2001) *Surviving your Dissertation: A Comprehensive Guide to Content and Process*, Newbury Park, CA: Sage.

Samraj, B. (2002) 'Texts and contextual layers: academic writing in content courses', in A.M. Johns (ed.) *Genre in the Classroom: Multiple Perspectives*, Mahwah, NJ: Lawrence Erlbaum.

Samraj, B. (2005) 'The generic structure of discussion sections in Master's theses', paper presented at the International Systemic Functional Conference, Sydney.

Scott, M. (1999) 'Agency and subjectivity in student writing', in C. Jones, J. Turner and B. Street (eds) *Students Writing in the University: Cultural and Epistemological Issues*, Amsterdam: John Benjamins.

Seliger, H. and Shohamy, E. (1989) *Second Language Research Methods*, Cambridge: Cambridge University Press.

Shaw, P. (1991) 'Science research students' composing processes', *English for Specific Purposes*, 10: 189–206.

Shen, F. (1989) 'The classroom and the wider culture: identity as a key to learning English composition', *College Composition and Communication*, 40: 459–466.

Silva, T. and Matsuda, P.K. (2002) 'Writing', in N. Schmitt (ed.) *An Introduction to Applied Linguistics*, London: Arnold.

Sinclair, M. (2005) 'The pedagogy of "good" PhD supervision: a national cross-disciplinary investigation of PhD supervision'. Available online at: <http://www.dest.gov.au/sectors/higher_education/publications_resources/profiles/pedagogy_of_good_phd_supervision.htm> (accessed 5 December 2005).

Starfield, S. (2003) 'The evolution of a thesis-writing course for Arts and Social Sciences students: what can applied linguistics offer?', *Hong Kong Journal of Applied Linguistics*, 8: 137–154.

Starfield, S. and Ravelli, L. (2006) '"The writing of this thesis was a process that I could not explore with the positivist detachment of the classical sociologist": self and structure in New Humanities research theses', *Journal of English for Academic Purposes*, 5: 222–243.

Stevens, K. and Asmar, C. (1999) *Doing Postgraduate Research in Australia*, Melbourne: Melbourne University Press.

Sung, C-I. (2000) 'Investigating rounded academic success: the influence of English language proficiency, academic performance, and socio-academic interaction for Taiwanese doctoral students in the United States', unpublished PhD dissertation, University of Michigan.

Swales, J.M. (1990) *Genre Analysis: English in Academic and Research Settings*, Cambridge: Cambridge University Press.

Swales, J.M. (1996) 'Occluded genres in the academy: the case of the submission letter', in E. Ventola and A. Mauranen (eds) *Academic Writing: Intercultural and Textual Issues*, Amsterdam and Philadelphia: John Benjamins.

Swales, J.M. (2004) *Research Genres: Explorations and Applications*, Cambridge: Cambridge University Press.

Swales, J.M. and Feak, C.B. (1994) *Academic Writing for Graduate Students*, Ann Arbor: University of Michigan Press.

Swales, J.M. and Feak, C.B. (2000) *English in Today's Research World*, Ann Arbor: University of Michigan Press.

Tardy, C.M. (2005) '"It's like a story": rhetorical knowledge development in advanced academic literacy', *Journal of English for Academic Purposes*, 4: 325–338.

Taylor, T.L. (2000) 'Women, sport and ethnicity: exploring experiences of difference in netball', unpublished PhD thesis, University of New South Wales. Available online at: <http://www.library.unsw.edu.au/~thesis/adt-NUN/public/adt-NUN20011012.144327/> (accessed 1 September 2006).

Thompson, D.K. (1993) 'Arguing for experimental "facts" in science: a study of research article results sections in Biochemistry', *Written Communication*, 10(1): 106–128.

Thompson, P. (1999) 'Exploring the contexts of writing: interviews with PhD supervisors', in P. Thompson (ed.) *Issues in EAP Writing Research and Instruction*, Reading: Centre for Applied Language Studies, University of Reading.

Thompson, P. (2005) 'Points of focus and position: intertextual reference in PhD theses', *Journal of English for Academic Purposes*, 4: 307–323.

Timms, W.A. (2001) 'The importance of aquitard windows in the development of alluvial groundwater systems: Lower Murrumbidgee, Australia', unpublished PhD thesis, University of New South Wales. Available online at: <http://www.library.unsw.edu.au/~thesis/adt-NUN/public/adt-NUN20030113.091215/> (accessed 12 September 2006).

Tinkler, P. and Jackson, C. (2000) 'Examining the doctorate: institutional policy and the PhD examination process in Britain', *Studies in Higher Education*, 25: 167–180.

Torrance, M.S. and Thomas, G.V (1994) 'The development of writing skills in doctoral research students', in R.G. Burgess (ed.) *Postgraduate Education and Training in the Social Sciences*, London and Bristol: Jessica Kingsley.

Turner, J. (2003) 'Writing a PhD in the contemporary humanities', *Hong Kong Journal of Applied Linguistics*, 8: 34–53.

Vande Kopple, W.J. (1985) 'Some exploratory discourse on metadiscourse', *College Composition and Communication*, 36: 82–93.

Waites, C.K. (1999) 'The professional life-cycles and professional development of adult teachers of English to speakers of other languages (TESOL)', unpublished PhD thesis,

University of New South Wales. Available online at: <http://www.library.unsw.edu.au/~thesis/adt-NUN/public/adt-NUN20011128.142410/> (accessed 12 September 2006).

Wakeling, L.K. (1998) 'Theorising creative processes in the writing of the neo-historical fiction Watermarks', unpublished PhD thesis, University of New South Wales. Available online at: <http://www.library.unsw.edu.au/~thesis/adt-NUN/public/adt-NUN2000.0012/> (accessed 12 September 2006).

Wallace, M. and Wray, A. (2006) *Critical Reading and Writing for Postgraduates*, London: Sage.

Wang, W. (2006) 'Editorials on terrorism in Chinese and English: a contrastive genre study', unpublished PhD thesis, University of Sydney.

Weissberg, R.C. and Buker, S. (1990) *Writing up Research: Experimental Research Report Writing for Students of English*, Englewood Cliffs, NJ: Prentice Hall Regents.

White-Davison, P.A.M. (1999) 'Rural views: schooling in small rural/remote communities', unpublished MPhil thesis, Griffith University. Available online at: <http://www4.gu.edu.au:8080/adt-root/public/adt-QGU20030303.140524/> (accessed 12 September 2006).

Winter, R., Griffiths, M. and Green, K. (2000) 'The "academic" qualities of practice: what are the criteria for a practice-based PhD?', *Studies in Higher Education*, 25: 25–37.

Wu, S. (2002) 'Filling the pot or lighting the fire? Cultural variations in conceptions of pedagogy', *Teaching in Higher Education*, 7(4): 387–395.

Yang, R. and Allison, D. (2003) 'Research articles in Applied Linguistics: moving from results to conclusions', *English for Specific Purposes*, 33: 365–385.

Zerubavel, E. (1999) *The Clockwork Muse: A Practical Guide to Writing Theses, Dissertations and Books*, Cambridge, MA: Harvard University Press.

Index